I0159239

A THOUSAND WORDS

Also by Jonathan Salem Baskin

Branding Only Works On Cattle

Bright Lights & Dim Bulbs

Histories of Social Media

With Sue Unerman:

Tell The Truth

A THOUSAND WORDS

Why We Must Fight the Tyranny of Brief, Vague & Incomplete

Jonathan Salem Baskin

Shadows on the Cave Wall

Chicago | London | Clavius Base

© 2013 Jonathan Salem Baskin

All rights reserved.

A Thousand Words:
Why We Must Fight the Tyranny
of Brief, Vague & Incomplete
By Jonathan Salem Baskin
ISBN: 0985182423
ISBN-13: 978-0985182427

First Edition: 2013

All rights reserved. No part of this book may be
reproduced or transmitted in any form or by any means,
electronic or mechanical, including photocopy, recording,
or any information storage retrieval system, without
permission in writing from the publisher, except brief
passages for review purposes.

Library of Congress Cataloguing in Publication Data:
A catalog record for this book is available
from the Library of Congress

For interviews, extended citations, or booking
information, please contact:

Shadows on the Cave Wall
P. O. Box 471
Glencoe, IL 60022 USA

TABLE OF CONTENTS

PART THREE: Writing Revolutions

PART FOUR: The Great Disconnect

PART FIVE: Finding Ourselves in the 21st Century

EPILOGUE

PROLOGUE:
THE NEW ELITISM

"A picture is worth a thousand words" means that images are fast, better communicators of meaning than text. This jibes with our everyday experience. We don't have to work to reach conclusions about imagery. Pictures are immersive and compelling in an unavoidable sort of way; they invite us to finish them with our own reactions, their truths self-evident because they trigger in us things we already know or believe. We don't have to learn how to look at them since we connect with them directly. Their meanings are obvious.

Many living things communicate visually. Bees share flower locations via complex dance routines. Schools of fish and formations of birds move in response to subtle nuances of gesture. Dogs and cats let us know when they're angry by baring their teeth, and obey the commands of human gestures (well, dogs do). Visual symbols are their language.

Other species don't *talk*. They sometimes react to visual or chemical stimuli with sounds, but they do so wordlessly. Though, like us, when they react to visuals it's usually with a single emotion, which is combined with a simple physical response, such as *run*, or don't *run*. As much as this enables them to communicate, they are enslaved to its blunt and mostly binary content. Most if not all of it is autonomic.

But we humans go further. We use words to shape, label, and store our thoughts. Explanations occur in words, not pictures, and usually add context and nuance to imagery, if not wholly changing our first impressions. We're the only species that has developed a complex set of symbols, each of which have meaning that can be combined to change meaning while also creating it anew. Words allow us to form complicated ideas as well as share and remember them. After all, the capacity to name things was God-given to Adam among all the species of the Garden of Eden. Words are the most robust and reliable information storage and transmission medium ever invented. Considering how early babies acquire linguistic skills, there's a good chance this capability is hardwired into our brains. Some have even theorized that words are required for consciousness itself.

Interestingly, words let us learn what's around, behind, and after images. They allow us to have conversations that continue long after the images are remembered or forgotten. We use words to articulate *questions* and comprehend *answers*, and to replace the immediacy of visceral reaction with more sustained and rich understanding. Images talk to our senses, but words exist as conversations of our minds. Without the detail and specificity required and enabled by words, images distract and mislead as often as they inform. Images imprison us in the moments we view them. They find home in our subjective experiences.

The truth is that an image is all but worthless without words, no matter how powerful or immediate it might feel.

Perhaps that's why institutions and the powerful throughout history have managed access to words (and then text) as a means of political and social control. More precisely, they preferred to skip them completely and instead rely on imagery and visual stimuli to assert their authority. The pomp of aristocratic life was intended as a visual marker for expected behavior. Rules of governance were expressed through the actions of heavily armed authorities. Gothic cathedrals were built to evoke fear and awe during the same time as religious texts were kept in Latin so the common folk couldn't read them. Slaves were kept illiterate in 1860s America for fear they would learn how to change their situation. Twentieth century totalitarian regimes from the Soviets to the Khmer Rouge did all they could to control the transmission of words in speeches or text, while emphasizing the "truths" of slogans and "realism" of state-created art.

The uses of imagery in commerce are also manipulative, if not so destructively. Advertising didn't enter its heyday until color magazines allowed for ads conceived as images, thereby abandoning the reasoned arguments they'd once made with words. Visuals of happy vacuum-cleaner owners evoke visceral responses among non-owners, not a debate about the relative merits of one device or another. *Keeping up with the Joneses* is a picture of an idea, not a thoughtfully articulated case. *Want this* is its blunt message. The success of television, like film before it, was a result of its ability to present vivid images. It's why we talk now about the power of YouTube videos and photos on Instagram. They communicate easily and fast, even if what they contain is often vaguely symbolic and incomplete.

Conversely, every major liberation movement in history has relied on words, whether the limit to aristocratic power evidenced by the *Magna Carta* in 1215, the literacy spurred by the Gutenberg press in the 15th century, or the knowledge made possible by Tyndale's translation of the <u>Bible</u> into common English a century later. This is why the proliferation of common, public education can be seen as the key driver of individual social mobility and success during the global transformation of the 19th century; reading (and writing) were its enabling mechanisms.

Yet we live in an age when these facts of history stay unmentioned and mostly misunderstood. Imagery has been elevated to supremacy as a communications vehicle, and words reduced to their briefest numbers and uses. If something can't be expressed in 140-characters or less, or summarized on a bulleted slide, then it's probably not worth communicating. We go to conferences to hear presentations in quippy 18-minute intervals and then celebrate their brevity. We bemoan government because legislation fills up too many pages of paper. Details dare our attention spans. Visual and short are better, whatever the circumstances. We've embraced our new communications without recognizing what we've given up.

These days, our use of words, text, and reasoned argument takes too much time. Worse, there's a new elitism that equates the briefest of communication with the smartest; substitutes quick declarations for reasoned conversation; and confuses visceral reaction with thoughtful truth. We obey the simplest of promises and dreams without considering what we forsake. We talk more but say less, choosing instead to value common sharing over individual creation. There's an entire theology that encourages us to consume and comment. We call it *new media*, and consider it an improvement.

We need to reacquaint ourselves with these two ways of perceiving the world, through images and with words, and explore how each affects what we know and do.

This book is about why we must fight the tyranny of brief, vague, and incomplete communications. It's a manifesto about the need to take back control of the ideas and words by which we learn and share. It will take more than pictures or tweets to build our future. It could take a thousand words.

PART ONE:
TWO WAYS TO EXPERIENCE THE WORLD

RECOGNITION

My cat is sitting behind my computer monitor as I type this sentence. Every morning, she jumps onto my desk and pokes around, checking the screen and backside connections as if she's just discovered them for the first time. A loud purr starts when she sniffs my face and rubs against my cheek before hopping back to the floor and moving to her next stop. She'll repeat this routine a few more times today. Each visit, it's clear that she knows me.

But does she? Science can't tell us for sure that cats, or any animals actually *remember* things, whether people or places, or simply *recognize* them. Think of it as the difference between a continuous experience through which she carries memories of things that are external to her compared to an endless series of discreet, disconnected *nows* in which she reacts to things presented to her.

Reacting is good descriptive for the way other living things interact with the world. Plants slowly turn to the sun when warmth hits their leaves. Monkeys warn one another about imminent danger. These behaviors don't evidence something called *object permanence,* and it might help explain why domesticated animals don't go nutty living in the same house or apartment year after year, walking the same pathways and doing the same things they do daily.

When my cat goes to explore the kitchen for the umpteenth time in her life, it's full of discoveries for her because it's unlikely she possesses a permanent mental image of the place when she's not in it. Rather, the moment she enters the room is not linked to the moment immediately prior (perhaps the doorway from the dining room). Her senses feed stimuli into her cat brain and she responds in the moment. The warm spot by the window above the sink is a good place to sit. There's a plastic bag on the counter that needs to be chewed.

She recognizes things, but she hasn't returned to a place that had an external existence in her consciousness. She didn't find the kitchen *again* as much as *anew* or, maybe better put, it's a new *now* until she passes through time to the next one. Her life is thus lived not as a series of returning to things she knows, but discovering them and then reacting. It's not that my cat forgets the kitchen every time she leaves it. She certainly recognizes me when our eyes meet and she meows. The kitchen and I simply stop existing when we're not a part of her sensory *now*. It's binary. On and off.

It might help to think of it as a matter of dimensions, as Edwin Abbott wrote in his 1884 novel <u>Flatland: A Romance of Many Dimensions</u>. His protagonist is a two-dimensional square living in a two-dimensional world of length and width in which his compatriots simply cannot fathom what a third dimension of height might be. It's not that they can't imagine it. The idea itself doesn't exist.

Continuity of experience is that third dimension that animals and plants lack, so the age-old question of does the falling tree make noise in the forest if nobody is there to hear it has particular resonance. My cat, or the smartest animal we could mention, isn't aware of the forest at all unless she's in it. She feels satisfied or safe with me, but doesn't experience those feelings *about me* when we're not together. She and animals in general lack the object permanence necessary to maintain those connections. We humans alone possess it.

If accurate -- and again, researchers still debate the science -- this has significant implications for animals' sense of self. In a sentence, they don't have one, and that's why visual stimuli (or other direct sensory inputs) suffice for communication.

All living things respond to sensory stimuli, whether their sensory apparatus are even apparent. Bacteria sense sugar in trace amounts without smelling or tasting it. Sperm use subtle chemicals to sense the direction in which they're swimming, and can change course accordingly. You can see that same base reflexive interactivity in human experience: we pull our hands away from fire, shudder in reaction to loud noises, and close our eyes when we look directly at the Sun. Those moments of experience are no different for us than they are for cats or bacteria.

But we are different from them. Without a sense of object permanence, animals have no sense of self, no "I" or "me" doing the reacting. We call them *reflexes*; they're automatic, like an oven beeping when a set temperature has been reached, or a track switch stopping two nearby trains from colliding. My cat certainly interacts with her environment, but she doesn't carry with her a continuing awareness of her self any more than she maintains a worldview of other things. She's *of* each moment, not *in* it. When she looks into a mirror, she doesn't see herself. She may not even see another cat.

This also makes for significant limitations to communication. There's little detail or nuance when animals communicate with one another. Their squawks, barks, and meows are inexorably a part of the moment, providing a direct reaction to it. *Fear. Safety. Status.* Even the dances or bees and foraging patterns of ants are of the moment, not a self-aware continuity imposed upon it. This makes learning difficult, and transmission of knowledge across generations all but impossible. My cat's behaviors would be identical to those of her ancestor cats thousands of years ago.

Some researchers believe that animals feel emotions (so maybe dogs really do miss their masters, and elephants bury their dead due to some dim awareness of their permanent loss). I'm not sure I agree or, if it's true, those feelings aren't also simply discreet moments of experience. *Sad* or *happy* could be less abstract ideals for them as much as tangible reactions to specific stimuli.

Maybe we can agree that living things have senses that are programmed to react to what we see, hear, taste, touch, and smell. Recognition is fast and immediate, just as it's blunt and fleeting. We sense something, and we respond.

Ah, my cat is back for another visit. She says *meow* to me, as if for the first time

CONSCIOUSNESS

Do you know what happens to you each night between the time you fall asleep and awake the next morning? You certainly have a good idea, of course: you spend it sleeping in your bed. It's where you sign off and rejoin the conscious world. The circumstantial evidence is pretty solid on that point. You might remember your dreams, but they don't take you someplace different, at least not physically. It might be entertaining to consider the possibilities -- your spirit walks high-power transmission lines, or you get up and play cards with other sleep-walkers in your household -- but the only one thing that's unequivocally certain is that you turn off your consciousness when you sleep, so you'll never really know. When you wake up every morning, you have to take it on faith that you're the same *you* who went to sleep the night prior.

Shutting yourself off and then turning yourself on again is a strange thought, isn't it? It means our experience of living is episodic, not continuous. We carry memories and expectations with us (that object permanence described in the last chapter), but they're inert within us when we're not accessing them. When our entire consciousness powers down every night, it takes with it that recorded content as well as our awareness of awareness itself.

Communicating throughout much of history was similarly episodic and somewhat discontinuous.

When we look at an image, we're experiencing the 'right now' of the moment captured in the frame. We're a part of it, in a moment that consists of both the image and our act of viewing. It is a unique, discreet event in which we react to the elements in the picture and assign meaning to them. It doesn't matter what the painter or photographer intended to communicate, since that information isn't contained in the image itself. If you have prior awareness of that information, you're less interacting with the image and more so looking for that pre-determined meaning. Taken on their own, images don't tell us as much as we tell ourselves when we look at them. The moment of viewing is also the moment to which we give it meaning.

As soon as we look away, however, the image loses all of that meaning, whether or not we commit our interpretation of it to memory. Visual stimuli themselves store no meaning; they're *prompts* for us to associate meaning to the elements we see. There's no explicit content in them beyond the frame of our vision -- the boundaries of the photo, painting, or video -- which is why no two people will react in the exact same way, nor will the same visuals necessarily prompt the same interpretation if you revisit them sometime in the future (if anything, they may prompt your recollection of your first reaction). Images are *triggers for communicating*, not vessels of communications content. Imagery carries with it no continuous meaning. A picture gallery is a *collection of possibilities.*

Verbal communication is somewhat similar, at least in its ephemeral quality. For our ancestors to hear something, they had to be within earshot of the speaker. Since most of them didn't move about much in their lifetimes, this meant that most of what they heard came from people they knew, or knew something about. You had to be aware of, if not overtly know, the speaker in order to hear what he or she had to say, which meant you brought prior data to bear on every verbal exchange. But everything else about it was real-time. When someone was done speaking, the transmission of content ended, the event was over, and the words lost to the past. Whatever was shared was stored mentally thereafter, but there was no external record of it. Making sounds is not unlike seeing things when it comes to both being in and of a moment. When the experience ends the communicating is shut down, like you've gone back to sleep.

Well, there was one major difference: spoken words contained the same meaning whether they were heard by one person, a crowd, or nobody at all. But spoken words evaporate in time irrespective of audience.

That transience and discontinuity changed when writing was invented. Writing severed the relationship between the moment of communicating and the creation of meaning and memory. Text has *inherent meaning*, so it allows for sharing and retention that endures, uninterrupted, irrespective of time, place, or witness. The meaning of writing goes beyond the experience of reading in a moment, and provides for a collective memory which anyone can access, any time. It can be stored somewhere other than your brain.

Writing is *code* that contains meaning. Letters combine to form words, and words are arrayed in sentences and paragraphs to build arguments and tell stories. You can decide how you feel about the content when you read it, and your reaction can be different each time you read, but the meaning is literally written into the words. Writing is self-referencing and complete, unlike visual stimuli that requires someone to assemble and interpret the elements into meaningful conclusions or reactions. A book is a book when you put it on your nightstand and then pick it up the next morning. It doesn't shut off any more than it awaits interpretation to have meaning. It just *is*.

Written communication is not dependent on place and time, and it doesn't rely on a reader having any prior knowledge of the writer or the topic. Your experience of reading will be qualified by what you know and who you are, of course, but the code of what's written is identical for everyone. The elements of visual expression, such as the items in a picture, also don't change from viewer to viewer, but their meaning only arises from the experiential moment of engaging with it. A picture of a wet dog is funny to one viewer and sad to another. Conversely, the words "In the beginning" are far more explicitly identical every time they're read. It's why more words mean it's more likely the conclusions will resemble one another across readings. Clarity of meaning is a variable contained in the written medium.

Writing meant that people could create and share information across space and time because we could rely upon its standardization and consistency. Again, reactions can always vary, as can understanding. But the medium itself was and is a vessel for content that isn't episodic or ephemeral. We know what people wrote thousands of years ago, while we have not a clue to how they completed the visual experience of public buildings or the gestures of kings and queens. We'll always react to imagery when it's in sight, but we've learned to outsource our consciousness to the written word before and thereafter.

This lets me write about things like sleep, or about my cat.

SPECIFICITY

We have no idea when people started talking to one another. They were probably grunting and grimacing for eons, but likely estimates for two-way, repeatable conversations puts the first moment at somewhere between 50,000 to 75,000 year ago. There's no recording available, of course; this also happens to be the approximate time when folks started building tools out of more than one material, and then improving them across the generations. A few million years of monosyllabic utterances had yielded no such advances in technology, but then the game abruptly changed, leading many experts to believe that the presence of language is a prerequisite for civilization itself.

There's less agreement on *how* language emerged. Did we first learn to mimic sounds in nature, for instance, or did the genetic predisposition of our visceral responses and vocal cords literally shape our communications? It's reasonable to assume that things started simply, perhaps with vocalizations to express approval, disapproval, happiness, and fear. Though no different from what many other species use to get schools, packs or flights moving in the right direction, our ancestors shared those vocal cues between brains that possessed the unique capacity to apply, aggregate, and retain that information. I've always found it interesting that our subspecies is named *homo sapiens sapiens*, as if to point out that we're the only animals aware of our own awareness.

I think language was and is the catalyst for this awareness, which is doubly intriguing since the first written communication was *visual*. Humans started drawing pictures of animals on the walls of caves in France and Spain nearly 40,000 years ago. Sometimes the imagery got rather complex, portraying entire scenes as if sketched from memory of actual experiences. Other times, elements were superimposed over one another like the pictures were meant to show movement across time. Scenes in the caves of Lascaux appear to tell stories of hunts, for instance. But they don't really *tell* anything the way we'd expect a language would.

The drawings were likely the backdrop to a multi-sensory experience involving sounds, torchlights, smells, and even physicality. The pictures were prompts for a larger, more varied and integrated participatory moment...*a shared picture* that would never be experienced or remembered the same way twice. You can just imagine people crowded together in one of those dark caves, with flashes of torchlight pulsing across animal drawings on the walls as if to suggest their very movement while the smoke made it harder to see and breath. The sound of chanting linking the storyteller with his or her audience. It must have been quite impactful. We may have been genetically programmed to respond to sensory experiences like it.

This *symbolic communication* was less like a written language, and more like a map or work of art. The sounds of everyday spoken language had to be far more explicit and repeatable, by definition, since they we used to accomplish things like teach stone tool manufacture, or warn the clan that a particular predator was approaching. Putting that level of specificity into writing emerged spontaneously in many places around the world starting in the mid-3000s BCE, or with the start of the Bronze Age (again, see the connection between language and developmental progress in civilization?). Cuneiform and hieroglyphics are literally "word pictures" that visually represent something that has some meaning, and that has been visually experienced. *It's a language of sights and memories, not code.* Interestingly, a closely controlled class of scribes who are able to read and write pops up concurrent with the use of writing in societies from China, to the Americas and the Middle East.

Written language made possible communication that was far more specific and reliably repeatable, which is why it was immediately confined to the purview of a small and guarded class of people who could use it. Ruling elites used it to assert ownership of property, such as declarations on stele posted on roads or in front of buildings. It was used to list possessions, which is why we find laundry lists in Egyptian tombs. Though we have prayers and the occasional fictional tome from this period, the primary use of written language was to enable commercial or governmental actions. Remember, regular people were all the while using ever-increasingly complex spoken languages to conduct their lives, too. Spoken words sufficed to maintain relationships with other adults, teach skills to their children, and build societies.

History's first words were prose, not poetry. And both spoken and written, they were a (if not *the*) medium of social understanding.

Finally, language written as we know it, using an alphabet of symbols that represented *phonemes*, or sounds, came on the scene with the start of the Iron Age. This is the period when long and detailed works of literature were produced, such as the Indian <u>Vedas</u> and Hebrew <u>Bible</u>, which go into excruciatingly detailed specificity to explain how the universe works. Greek tragedies do something similar as they plum the depths of the human heart, and Rome's Latin oratories capture the political maneuvering of its republican leaders. Literacy was still reserved for the select few, but the utility of words -- constructed out of letters that can be arranged to communicate just about any thought or command -- found its way into aspects of daily life. Tombstones noting names and life accomplishments first appear in Rome during this time.

This approach to language -- words composed of letters -- is the code that pictograms were not and, as such, it became the true software on which civilization has been built and run ever since. Societies became more accomplished and complex, so did their spoken and written languages, perhaps the latter enabling the former as much as serving as its narrative tool. Words are specific in the same way that visual communication is general, and make possible not just the transmission of ideas across time and space but also the invention of said ideas. Words give us the capacity to define things and one another, using words to do so (and not using them only to express the sensory stimuli we experienced). Their power cannot be underestimated.

As John 1:1 declares, as if to affirm the very mechanism of God's creation, "In the beginning, there was the word."

CONTRASTS

Images and words are two very different ways of experiencing the world, different ways of learning and sharing knowledge. Both seem to be hardwired into our physiology and play important roles in the development and uses of communication. In many ways they are diametrically opposite, however, and understanding these contrasts is important to understanding how each influences our lives today.

Images are **fast**/words are **slow**. Our minds process visual stimuli almost instantaneously, as we perceive the *whole* of a visual setting (*gestalt theory* in psychology posits that our brains are wired to perceive entire settings before we recognize individual parts). Reading is *linear*, one word at a time, and any given sentence may not reveal its meaning until completed (or a larger idea after a paragraph or more). The act of reading slows down the processes of comprehension. Seeing takes no time. Reading demands it.

Images are **intuitive**/words are **learned**. Animals respond to visual stimuli without any preparation, and human beings almost can't avoid drawing conclusions from imagery that range from visceral to more complex. Seeing isn't *taught*. Words have to be learned. Language is a cognitive step beyond sensation. Words themselves have objective definitions. No image possesses a standard or accepted meaning.

Images are **holistic**/words are **linear**. Just like the "whole" of the moment described earlier, visual stimuli is correlative; an image consists of a number of elements that combine to produce meaning. The meaning of those elements changes depending on individual circumstance (i.e. how they're assembled). Words are read in a specified order. Other than gasping at length, there's nothing a sentence tells you until you read it. You can skip to the last sentence in a paragraph but you'll risk getting no more than a taste of what you missed.

Images **telegraph meaning**/words **compile it**. Studying an image can often reveal more detail and nuance, but visuals usually instantly telegraph their main or blunt meaning. We "get" pictures, and once we've seen them they don't provide additional content (you can look again, but it won't necessarily tell you more). Words must be compiled, whether in real-time as they're heard, or over time when they're read. Reading builds arguments, layering the next point or detail upon the last. Your perspective on it changes when you get to each new sentence or idea. The more you read, the more you get.

Images are **real-time**/words **pause time**. Looking at something isn't a process, it just happens, in that perceiving visually is a real-time experience that involves whatever is presented in the moment (i.e. *looking*). People form opinions and recollections therefrom. Reading requires focused attention, to the exclusion of other activities, and then requires further processing. It's not dependent on the circumstances of the moment. Visual stimuli are *of* time. Reading *consumes it.*

Images are **shared experience**/words are **solitary**. People can look at the same thing at the same time. Participants actually add to the moment they're experiencing, in that presence and conclusions of *witnesses* can change the experience of the moment. While two or more people can read the same words at the same time, they're not collaborating on the experience (unless they're creating another level of interaction, like talking about what they're reading). Most readers are detached from their immediate surroundings, including the visuals therein.

Images are **emotional**/words are **rational**. Perhaps because of our evolution, visual stimuli seems to have a direct connection to our emotions, so we immediately and often unconsciously attach emotive labels to what we see: *good*, *bad*, *scary*, whatever. Our reactions are visceral. Reading makes no such link to our feelings. We might develop emotive responses to what we read, but those reactions are cognitive conclusions. We *decide* what and how we feel about words.

Images are **one-way**/words are **two-way**. This might seem counterintuitive at first blush, but imagery is one-way because it just *is*. Whether the imagery is organic or contrived, you either react to it or you don't. There is a limited and set amount of content in visual stimuli (defined by what's contained within the boundaries of the frame of sight and circumstance of the moment). There is no such thing as *organic text*. Words need to be arranged by someone with the intention of communicating something(s). Readers have the capacity and authority to agree or disagree with every element they read. Writers *talk to us*, by definition, and we talk back, even if only with the voices in our heads. Visuals have impact. Reading conveys meaning.

Just consider your experience reading the words of this chapter so far. You could have looked at an image far more easily, or perceived visual stimuli in real experience in a fraction of that time. Your reactions would have been almost immediate, simple, and obvious. Instead, you read what I've written and, line by line, interacted with me. One point made sense. Another didn't. The next one prompted a few additional thoughts, and then I followed it with a point that you felt wasn't terribly insightful.

I built my case and you vetted it, contemplating what I am saying. The experience wasn't and isn't simple or obvious, and it kept you from doing something else. Whether you like what I've written or think it's utter rubbish, there's no easy way to share it with someone else. You can share your *reaction* via words -- "it's brilliant" or "he sucks" -- but for someone else to perceive what I've written, they have to have read the words, too.

There is vastly more information contained in textual vs. visual content. There's no way a picture or video takes the place of words. Images and words are different ways of communicating. Both experiences allow us to interact with the world and one another.

Not better or worse, just very different.

PART TWO:
THE MECHANICS OF POWER

AUTHORITY

In a world in which we only learn and know through what we perceive immediately through our five senses, the concept of *authority* possess specific geophysical dimensions. That's why the earliest religions were based on nature's sights, sounds, and smells, which literally spoke with unequivocal and obvious power. Thunder and lightening. The blinding rays of sunrise. The darkness of a forest. An array of stars glowing in the sky. These stimuli were personified and given names, and the visceral emotions they prompted assigned to cosmic purposes without the need for much if any interpretation. The messages of the gods were big and loud. Believers saw them in the sights of churning waves and tumbling clouds.

Since they emerged from physical forces, people tied them to *places* on Earth. The first churches were carved in natural formations of rock and river. Temples were founded on mountaintops, and holy places sited deep inside caves. Most of the places associated with supernatural authority were set apart from the locations of everyday experience, too. They looked different than the places at which people normally congregated and access to them was limited.

The visuals of *place* were also used to assert authority by the wealthy and powerful in early societies. The idea of a home having *curb appeal* is thousands of years old; aristocrats in ancient Rome didn't build large homes only because they could afford the space, but because the physical presence of such homes advertised their status. The fact that most of those urban dwellings had rooms oriented around an inner courtyard hidden from street view meant that access to such places of power was limited, just like it was to those locations that had religious authority. *Bigger* and *restricted* meant *more authoritative*, if not simply more powerful (often the same thing throughout history). The physical spaces controlled by the wealthy weren't just expressions of fashion or culture, but tools of governance and, as such, social control.

Actually, the imagery of fashion and other cultural artifacts have always been used to assert authority. The regalia of nobility, such as crowns and scepters, are intended for just that purpose, as are the fabrics of expensive clothes: silk and satin were reserved for the exclusive use of the upper classes in Elizabethan England. *Sumptuary statues* reserved the color purple and sable fur for the rulers, while gold, silver, and pearl embroidery were reserved for the use of dukes, marquises and earls. Carriages and servant retinues were to earthly authority what natural phenomena were to religion. They required no explanation or proof. Like natural phenomena, the reign of monarchs and the authority aristocrats enjoyed in society were literally god(s)-given rights. Anybody could see it. No other explanation was required.

Just try to imagine a cloudy, perhaps drizzly late afternoon in Paris sometime in the mid-1300s. The street is crowded with a cacophony of sights, sounds, and smells, none of which are particularly pleasing but instead combine to form a wash of sensory noise through which you must wade as much as walk. Then, Notre Dame appears before you. The structure is immense, bigger than anything else you will ever encounter in your entire life. The details of the structure are so many and complex that you can't follow them visually. The walls and buttresses practically climb into the sky! As you approach it, the building just gets bigger and more imposing. By the time you reach the entrance you are all alone. You walk inside to an interior space that reveals itself to you slowly. You're enveloped by its enormity and its silence. The room stretches as far as you can see, with arches and statues going every which way as they extend and then fade into a smoky hazy that lingers at the level of enormous stained glass windows. You are struck speechless, your head bowed, which is exactly what you're supposed to do. You've reacted viscerally to the symbol of the cathedral, and it has told you the blunt point you need to know...even if you can't fully articulate it.

Just as cathedrals were communications tools that combined medium and message, so were the homes and trappings of the elite. Had you neared a gaggle of aristocrats on your way home from Notre Dame, their clothing and carriages would have announced not only their status, but what behavior was expected of you. Visual authority was immediate and unequivocal. The visual language of authority also had associative value, insomuch that priests and retainers wore uniforms to identify themselves with their sources of power (coats of arms were created to allow members of aristocratic households to literally *wear their colors*).

Another important quality of visual authority is that it precluded questioning. There is no way to debate with the physical structure of an immense church, especially considering an illiterate penitent was still likely aware that the truths underlying the institution were written somewhere out of reach, literally and figuratively. Rank-and-file citizens were purposefully barred from learning to read so as to maintain this status quo. Monks, scribes, and poets or other artists who could be bought by the wealthy were the keepers of written content, just as they'd done so since writing was first invented. It's interesting to note that much of the written output in the early centuries of the Dark Ages was almost visual in its expression, too; pages of vellum or parchment were laboriously illustrated, as if even pages of text were rendered as pictures. We are hardwired to react to visual stimuli.

But writing rarely if ever entered into the experience of most peasants. They were limited to the blunt authoritative communications of imposing cathedrals and regalia of wealth to which there was no response other than deference. There was no dialogue or discussion with a palatial home or bodyguards standing between peasant and aristocrat. The visual information was set, the data perceived by eyesight and perhaps augmented by other senses established. Peasants could only *react* to the stimuli, They had no capacity to say something *to* or *with* it. In this way, visual authority was *announced answer*, not *argued case*.

We puny human beings cannot hope to respond to the jarring sound of a thunderclap emanating from a churning grey sky, or to presume to be recognized (let alone heard) before a choir of singers' voices swirling through the immense walls of a cathedral or aristocrat's hall.

We simply fall on bended knee in the very pesence of this authority.

COMMERCE

In commerce, a contract is both a prediction and self-fulfilling prophecy. It can describe past actions, present circumstances, and future plans. Its contents are made real by mutual assent and therefore have a force or authority that can be exerted in other places and times.

It's interesting to think about commerce as a communications medium. Any agreement is a contract, whether or not with legal sanction, isn't it? Promissory notes, shares of stock, or even conversations over handshakes that allow two or more otherwise strangers to define value and trade are rich bundles of communications content, with meaning and implications that go far beyond the mechanics of transacting.

I'm convinced that spoken and then written language not only emerged as ways to transfer technological know-how across distances, but were put to use enabling society itself.

Here's my logic: civilization is based on cooperation, and cooperation is *commerce*. People live together because they can transact with one another, then around that collaboration are built the economics, laws, philosophies, and cultural artifacts that constitute society. If I'm right, commerce worked around, in spite of, and as the populist remedy to the symbolic communication of visual authority.

The way commerce is driven by the specificity of words and numbers is a stark contrast to the generalities of image and symbol on which religious and aristocratic institutions relied. A visual image is nothing more than a description wedded to a specific place and moment in time. Because commerce is a *conversation* -- like tangoing, transactions take two -- it's the opposite of the one-way and intuitive consumption of visual content.

Maybe that's why it was long considered inappropriate for the rich or religious to practice anything commercial (French nobles before the Revolution were legally barred from working). Did such actions risk challenge to their authority, which was expressed through visual imagery that was mostly established and static? Whatever words were used to describe that power were kept as guarded secrets, the books and documents interpreted occasionally through sanctioned representatives who communicated in set ways.

Conversely, the conversations of commerce are never set, always evolving, and can belong to anyone. Imagery has long been shared as a part of it, if not imperfectly, but transactions have never really relied on it. For most of history, there was no way to exactly (or realistically) render images of merchandise. Signage was laughably crude. Illustrations were poorly rendered, providing less representations of products and more simply suggesting shape and form. Any buyer in a transaction who chooses to fill in meaning or details to a proffered image risks being surprised or disappointed, whether then or now.

When people transacted, they detailed the parameters of their conversations and could choose to agree or disagree. Details of these conversations were among the first things chiseled in stone and then painted on papyrus. Medieval marketplaces were conducted primarily in spoken language, but rudimentary records of transactions exist from as early as the 13th century (the ledgers of government tax collectors go back further).

Written communication grew in importance as trade networks expanded and the types and numbers of products and services multiplied. Words were what literally "filled in the blanks" of whatever visual representation was used, if any. *Commerce was the first social media* because it empowered people to collaborate with one another (using spoken language). Words allows people to collaborate.

In doing so, the words through which commerce was conducted enabled a new source of authority that was conceived differently than the one-way visual authority of religion and government elites. Words got things done, and they were reliable. Most political and social vows were converted from spoken to text as soon as literacy allowed. People wanted to capture more and more detail that could be objectively experienced, shared, and understood. It's how commerce gave rise to social governing systems that blew up the authority of old religious and aristocratic institutions.

Imagine that peasant leaving Notre Dame one day, or perhaps his local tax collector's office, and having not just the audacity but the tools to not only wonder why but articulate his demands for answers.

Considering the importance of words in any collaboration, the rule of language was usually the *more*, the *better*. It isn't by chance that legal documents are usually longer than anyone cares to read. It's only through detail that information can be specified and then relied upon. Length of written communication was not historically understood as a tool for obfuscation, at least not inherently, but rather it correlated with a greater intention and likelihood that parties would understand what they were transacting. A long-winded communication wasn't bad, necessarily. Sure, shorter bursts of written communication were sometimes unavoidable, as in early newspaper ads which were limited by available space and thus *classified* to group products and services into categories to give readers a better understanding of what was being sold. There are legal exceptions, too: America's purchase of the Louisiana Territory from France was accomplished with a 9-page hand-written treaty.

But business and political communicators in general would have laughed at the idea that shorter written communication was anything but vague and incomplete. Less written data meant a more likely reliance on visual (or other) stimuli, which would have lower objectively meaningful content that could be open to differing interpretation, and thereby possibly suffer from purposeful manipulation.

It's no surprise that words are the primary communications medium on the Internet, despite the technology's great ability to share video and audio. Unlike visual stimuli, words aren't inherently interesting or fun to see, but they are code for meaningful content that *could* be interesting. Pictures speed around the word via the social media technology platform *du jour*, and friends like and forward videos that made them laugh or cry, but the substance of commerce -- of transacting not just merchandise but ideas -- is conducted with words This hasn't changed from the way they were used thousands of years ago. We have at our disposal infinitely better visual representations of what we might buy or sell, but we still rely on words to communicate and cooperate.

Words replace the visual authority of old institutions with the authority of reasoned argument.

PATIENCE

Less than a third of the population of Elizabethan London could read (women far less often then men), and of that number even fewer had need to write more than their names on the occasional legal document. The media they consumed amounted the snippets of the <u>Bible</u> used to teach literacy in petty and grammar schools, augmented by longer passages read aloud in churches on Sundays and the secular posters used to make announcements, promote public events, and encourage people to buy tickets for the relatively new live theater industry.

Yet thousands of these not-too literate people would willingly crowd into a standing room-only pit before a stage, paying a penny and often skipping work in order to cheer, sob, and otherwise participate in regular performances of the plays by William Shakespeare.

How is it that today's better-educated audiences can't find the patience to endure, let alone enjoy and understand, even the first few lines of *Hamlet* or *Henry V*?

Of course, there are many exceptions, but it's safe to say that what was the epitome of popular entertainment in the late 16th century is an acquired taste in ours. What was to them a three-hour engaging pleasure is to us all but an unimaginable chore. We're comforted by assurances that our biology limits our attention spans to three minutes (or less), almost freed by the idea that we're not supposed to possess the capacity to focus for too long. Therefore, we're not supposed to appreciate anything that takes time to appreciate. But their proclivities illustrate that we're certainly capable of it.

The question is why we don't, and whether not doing so makes us smarter, more aware, or better off.

Evolutionary psychology posits that we're wired to recognize patterns, even when none exist. Our senses are tools for assessing situations, as if to enable us to make quick judgments and take action. Considering our ancestors lived in small tribes in which feedback was immediate, and those assessments meant avoidance of imminent danger or realization of reward, the theory makes sense. We have been bred to possess the capacity to make fast decisions. But our bias toward it is learned. Sensation is the result of adaptive learning. We've taught ourselves to regularly apply our considerable abilities to draw only quick conclusions.

Visual stimuli are particularly good for such cognition. There is a theory in neuroscience called *feature integration theory that* suggests that when we perceive things, we immediately add them to a picture of perception; a "whole," or integrated experience that defines, quite literally, where our consciousness resides. So we draw pictures of place and time, instinctively putting them together from the individual bits, memes, or various sensory data that we encounter. Everything we sense fits into this emergent whole, even when things don't quite fit neatly or completely. The pictures we see are the pictures we construct, not simply the reality presented to us.

We are genetically predisposed to short-cut to clarity, and so it feels good, intellectually and viscerally. Making faster decisions is easier when they're based on less information because details usually require more contemplation, which means we risk reaching conflicted or more nuanced conclusions. Less data mean simpler and therefore more complete pictures. So while it takes

Hamlet practically forever to give his "To be or not to be?" monologue, he ends up providing no conclusive answer to his question. It's a far easier idea to express it as a tweet and then simply like or forward with a *LOL*.

Perhaps this is why so much of today's online social dialogue defaults to extremes of positive or negative opinion. It's our genetic *fight or flight* perception tool applied to every conversation. We put pieces into our cognitive whole by labeling them with obvious tags. *Stupid. Smart. I like. I hate.* Our opinions are more *certain* when they're more *extreme* because there's less to them. We see black and white far more easily than we ever did shades of grey, so now we don't take the time to look for grey at all. It's like we talk in pictures, not words.

The same rules of science and genetics applied to life in the England of the late 1500s, yet people lived very differently than we do. In those differences are keys to the reasons why regular folks loved their Shakespeare.

The kids who got an education spent far more time doing so than we do. Days started earlier and ended later, during which grammar school students laboriously struggled their way through their Latin. Often only quasi-literate, they were forced to speak words more often than read them, which meant they learned how to rely on understanding language in real-time (that's why many of Shakespeare's double-entendres and other witty wordplay worked). People then sat through interminable spoken sermons in churches every Sunday and, since their immortal souls were at stake, they learned how to patiently pay attention. They learned to favor detail over brevity, and to find meaning in more content, not less of it.

Just imagine the crowd in the open-air Globe Theater, most of them having paid the price of a mug of ale for the chance to stand pressed against one another, chewing on nuts and dropping the shells to be crushed underfoot for hours they laughed, cried, and often yelled at characters during a performance. They were engaged in ways we moderns can't fathom. Their experience was made possible in large part because they'd developed the skills for patience that their genetics enabled. That's why they not only understood Shakespeare's plays, but enjoyed them.

For them, communicating was a *process*, not just a *moment*, and its experience yielded nuance that made plays like *Hamlet* far more than a tweetable plot outcome. Words added up to meanings greater than the sum of their vocabulary parts. That's why all of the world's great religions encourage *patience*; it's not a virtue of inherent value, but rather a tool for understanding. Patience has long been considered a learned skill for recognizing the patterns around us, and then weaving them together into coherent, integrated pictures that are ever-changing (as we change also). It's what we expected "smart" people to do, and it's what even the behavior that "regular folks" at Will's latest debut could evidence. They knew that bigger, more meaningful, and arguably more real patterns can only be perceived if you take the time and apply the skills to use the words that make that perception possible.

Knowledge is greater than the sum of the parts upon which we build it. Consumption of content can be fast, but patience is the time we allow for understanding it.

TYPE

The movable type Gutenberg's printing press relied upon in the mid-15th century was made possible with the birth of the Roman alphabet over a thousand years earlier.

Prior written languages had been *pictograms;* cuneiform and hieroglyphics were based on images that conveyed meaning through resemblance to physical objects. They were actually symbols referencing entire ideas that had been shared in experience. There was no way to tell what they meant simply by looking at them without also knowing their context, and little need to print since there were few who could read. This fact, combined with the cumbersome nature of early language, meant that the printing press found limited use in China, even though it had been invented there hundreds of years before Gutenberg independently arrived at the same idea.

Not surprisingly, early inscriptions in both the East and West were often numeric, evidencing a shared need for tracking information used in commerce or objects stuffed into burial chambers. Numbers connoted simple, direct, and self-referencing meaning. We invented them before the earliest written language.

The Latin alphabet we use today traces its origins to the Phoenicians, who came up in the 14th century BCE with the concept of individual symbols (each associated with a sound) and then assembling them into words that possessed inherent meaning. The Greeks borrowed their script and added vowels, which made it easier to speak words and do so quickly. They created the first actual written language. The Romans adapted it, and then spread Latin around the world.

Since writing is made possible by prior knowledge of letter-sounds, not awareness of entire picture symbols, it's easier to learn and use. It also maps with spoken language. Therefore, the places where Latin was spoken were where it was also most likely read, though one didn't guarantee the other. Reading is a learned behavior compared to seeing or listening. Where images can be sensed and spoken words understood, letters have no intrinsic meaning until they're taught, like numbers.

There's no consensus on how many words comprised the ancient Greek or Roman dictionaries, but they numbered many tens of thousands...far more than any single individual could have possessed or used. Words became a broad and deep resource from which writers could assemble concepts and arguments, some of which had quite literally never been said before.

Once written, these arguments became timeless for the same reasons that images and sounds aren't. Words don't lose their meaning when they fade or dissipate, because they aren't symbols of things but *the very code of meaning itself.* Copy may smudge, but if it's legible at all, it's still the same text, the same idea. The oratory of Cicero is as fresh today as it was when he first wrote his speeches because we can read the exact same words he used. Spoken in a high or low voice, fast or slow, they are unchanged from the time he chose to assemble and array them in a particular order.

The infinitely variable tool of spoken words invariably got locked down by the media and traditions available to the ancient world. It took time, money, and expertise to chisel them onto stele or the pediments of public buildings or, later, inscribe them on vellum, so the words committed to text were limited and chosen based on perceived social need. Overlaid on the vibrant sounds of conversations in homes and marketplaces were were text of government pronouncements and religious edicts. Writing was literally etched in stone, then inscribed by monks onto ornate pages of books that were closely guarded and infrequently copied, or carved into wood and pressed to create short books also known as *incunabula*.

Writing wasn't rendered mobile until the mid-1440s, when Johannes Gutenberg built his first printing press. His innovation wasn't the press, which had been used to produce books for many years, nor the use of ink or paper: it was *movable type*. Gutenberg had worked as a goldsmith and was familiar with melting and mixing various metals. He also understood the uses for punches and other molding tools. The movable type he created -- almost three hundred different letters, ligatures and punctuations -- was comprised of an alloy of antimony, lead, and tin. It meant that type could be arranged to produce any words or word order.

This innovation broke the connection between presenter and the content being presented. Though pages would continue to be decorated and colorized for centuries, the focus had been shifted to the text itself. His first products were printed indulgences for local churches and then a calendar, but soon a bible was in the works. More books would follow, as would more printers, as writing began its slow evolution from a medium that could be possessed, like a thing or object, to become something that had been freed to be *consumed* by readers. Literacy skyrocketed as people could experience ideas first-hand the words of Martin Luther or Erasmus, and not have to rely on the verbal paraphrasing or interpretation of others.

This freedom of expression was made possible by the versatility of the Latin alphabet, with its individual symbols literally "atoms" that could be rearranged into endless combinations that broke apart ideas into a constituent code of communicating. Written letters had always been movable, by definition of how the code was structured, so type was less a leap of invention than an application of an extant idea to the emergent technology of printing. Type was movable because letters always had been, at least conceptually.

The physical act of printing imbued books with a tactile sense of *movement*. Letter shapes pounded into paper retained the depression made when Gutenberg's device first pressed them. They were conceived with flecks at the ends of lines, called *serifs*, appearing like the marks left by the whacks of chisels. Letters were separate from one another, in stark contrast to the fluid lines of hand-written script, as if to remind readers that nobody really owned them. Words were by definition written by someone, but their constituent letters belonged to everyone, in every time.

Once printed, words never stopped moving.

PART THREE:
WRITING REVOLUTIONS

ARGUMENTS

We hate the endless stream of words that come from politicians today. The Conventional Wisdom is that there's too much talk and not enough action. There's also a question about the sincerity (or outright truthfulness) of what politicians say. Yet there'd be no politics -- which would mean no governance, laws, or social order -- without words. Historically, more words were actually better, however difficult that might be to believe. Words enabled people to communicate and thereby overcome the tyranny of blunt and vague authority that had been communicated by the edifices and practices of the rich and anointed. Words blew up the power of visual symbols, and the political tool to do so was the *reasoned argument*. The American Revolution is a good illustrative case for this point.

It was a war of words.

While transcendentalist essayist Ralph Waldo Emerson would almost 60 years later label the start of outright hostilities "the shot heard 'round the world," I'd suggest the real conflict was begun and then fought with words. Writing documents was a real-time endeavor for the colonial legislators, less as narrative of the burgeoning hostilities and more as an explanation for them, as well as a directional guide to their evolving argument with Britain. They would *win* because they proved they could explain not only why they believed they were right, and what their aspirations were, but then articulate the form of their ensuing governance.

By 1774, a split with the Mother Country was obvious, as various royal offices in the colonies were ransacked, folks refused to pay the various taxes Britain's Parliament insisted on imposing (staging the Boston Tea Party, for starters), and the states had organized their first collective governing body and named it the *First Continental Congress*. It got to work detailing in writing their grievances and hopes for reconciliation with Britain. Its *Petition to the King* was finalized on October 26, 1774, and came in at 2,112 words of what appeared to be sincere argument. Parliament's response was drafted about four months later; named the *Conciliatory Resolution*, it used all of 198 words to say, in effect, tough luck.

The battles of Lexington and Concord were fought two months later.

Then, Congress drafted a 1513-word opinion to articulate their point-by-point issues with Parliament's resolution (credited to Lord North, Britain's Prime Minister, and an outspoken opponent of colonial rights), and then another petition to King George III, informally known as the *Olive Branch Petition,* which came in at 1357 words on July 8, 1775. They must have expected its refusal, though, as the legislators also penned a longer, 2597-word explanation of why they would need to go to war, entitled *Declaration of the Causes and Necessity of Taking Up Arms.*

The British played true to form, issuing an 848-word Declaration of Rebellion on August 23, 1775 which succinctly announced that the colonies were at war with *them*. More fighting followed. It would take another six months of debating before an initial 1338-word *Resolution of Independence* would be proposed on June 7, 1776. The final *Declaration* followed a month later. Endless newspaper articles would cover every possible tidbit on the debate up to that point (and beyond).

It might seem quaint or somehow immaterial that legislators spent so much time debating their points and committing them to paper, but it was central to the concept of the American Revolution as a reasoned, collective action. It based the conflict in words, not just emotions, and required of its proponents a thoughtful commitment of time and intellect. The war may have played out on the battlefields of North America, but why it was fought, and what was established in its aftermath was decided in meeting rooms in Philadelphia and London. It was important that everyone knew what they were fighting about. Writing was the medium through which this meaning was established and conveyed.

This wasn't the first time that populist political actors used words to assert authority. In European history, you can go back to the days of the *Charter of Liberties* in early 12th Century England, which was King Henry I's attempt to specify in writing some limitations to his power and would lead to the creation of the *Magna Carter* by his barons a century later. Matin Luther's *95 Theses* in 1522 were a detailed, written argument against the symbolic authority wielded by the Catholic Church. Contrast such communication with the presumed inherent authority of a scepter or crown, the structure of a church's walls, or the very existence of a national army. The causality and specificity of reasoned arguments are the proven antidotes to the weight of authority that's presumed to be god-given or a fact of life.

Successful revolutions, whether political or commercial, need *scripts*, not just icons or slogans.

I'd offer that the lack of a detailed script is why the French Revolution went so far off the rails. The 824 words (in translation) of its *Declaration of the Rights of Man* were soaringly vague and lacked detail on how they'd be realized, leaving it to unelected groups and a series of interpreters who translated it into acts of violence for years. Different people interpreted it differently, just as they would a picture. Many of its assertions, such as individuals having the right to determine directly the function of government, were simply ill-conceived. It was *document as symbol*, or as an ideal; people killed one another "defending it" while violating its very principles through their actions. Conversely, scripts are how many of the union movements around the world in the late 19th century were so successful. They spelled out what they intended to do, why, and how.

In fact, there's somewhat of a direct correlation between the amount of detail in a written document, and people's ability to not only understand it but have a reasonable expectation of sharing those conclusions. Successful political (and commercial) events were constructed from reasoned arguments, not impromptu imagery, no matter how compelling. Throughout history, if you'd suggested that "brief was better," or said "if you can't tell me what the idea in a sentence or two, it's not worth my time," you would have been laughed at.

Even though consumers rely today on mostly visual and brief content for their decision-making, our public and private institutions are still based on bodies of written documentation that define how governments legislate, what things corporations can and can't do, and how public and private critics will judge and track those actions. It's their true source of power, not the buildings that house them, or the other symbols of their authority. That's why the Occupy Wall Street protests of 2011, while visually compelling, provided no sustainable authority. They gave no specific, credible alternate argument apart from producing compelling visual imagery. Same for the protests during the Iranian election a few years ago, or even some of the violent challenges to other governments in the Middle East. The pictures of protestors being beaten or rebel soldiers ducking for cover prompts immediate emotions of empathy or disdain, but they possess no thoughtful argument or explanation (other than the glib analyses of 'experts' on cable TV or posting anonymously on the same social platforms that propagated the images in the first place).

Images are no substitute for reasoned written argument, but rather blunt, vague, emotional conclusions. It's why fighting is considered the last and lowest form of argument. It's the shell or outline of debate, or evidence of the lack of one altogether. When we have no patience for extended conversation in lieu of outright violence, we're either being stupid or just lying to ourselves. Imagery is not a tool for real conversation, and collaboration requires words, patience, and contemplation.

Words are the only tools that allow us to argue about politics or commerce, or anything else. They're also the only way we reach understanding and agreement.

ADVERTISING

Advertising isn't a fact of life or force of nature. The practice was invented over time, based on circumstances and needs. For most of human history, nobody ever thought to create it (and the wherewithal didn't exist to deliver it). Advertising emerged as a byproduct of writing and printing and, in doing so, changed the way commerce was conducted. But paid commercial speech wasn't what we think of today; advertising was first and foremost a mechanism for sharing and vetting content. I know it sounds crazy, but advertising came into being as a tool to help people discover *the truth*. It used to empower more than it manipulated us.

We've been buying and selling with one another since ancient times. While commerce empowered us, too, trade was never considered particularly respectable. It was commonly expected that merchants were dishonest or would cut every conceivable corner. Business wasn't polite in the days of open stalls and marketplaces filled with the cacophony of sights and sounds, as sellers did their best to sell their wares through loud outcry and wild promises. *Caveat emptor*, or "buyer beware," is a Latin phrase that originated in medieval Europe, but you can imagine it applying to what went on in the *tabernae* stalls in Roman forums, too. In societies where there weren't many regulations to monitor transactions, let alone police forces to enforce laws, you truly took your life into your own hands every time you shopped.

Remember, medieval peasants weren't really consumers or shoppers. They were, well, *peasants*. They lived lives defined by an incessant struggle to survive, not making choices of personal taste and expression among endless opportunities like we do. While there is some research to suggest that craftsmen actually didn't work as many hours/day -- and thus had more free time -- they had no expectation for betterment through buying or possessing things, no linear mythology or economy for financial or social advancement. Their world was imagined as a giant wheel in which each individual had a set place. So there was no need for something like advertising to convince people what they *wanted*, since peasants were occupied finagling what they knew they *needed*.

Trust was rare in the 1600s and for quite some time thereafter. It was a given that butchers slipped unacceptable meats into their sausages and pies; bakers filled their bread and cakes with less wholesome substances; cobblers were stingy with nails, and seamstresses were intent on saving thread; and ale and other drinks were particularly suspect, whether cut with variety of substances or, like any fresh product, sold far beyond the date at which the words *turned* or *rotten* would apply.

It wasn't just that sellers weren't to be trusted. People didn't like the very nature of transactions effected with money. It was something unclean and unlike the local, more cordial and personal barter economies they remembered from their pasts, or from stories. Transacting was unavoidable, though, as more and more people populated the world's cities, and even rudimentary transport meant that some products were sold across ever-wider distances. Commerce was a necessary evil, with friends or strangers, because it allowed people to get what they needed.

There was little to no advertising up to this time other than public notices and verbal promise-making. People shared their experiences, and this knowledge affected future decision-making. Remember, most folks didn't travel far their entire lives, so the vast majority of sellers were held at least somewhat accountable for their promises, or consumers adjusted their expectations based on past experience. Therefore commerce, like conversations, was *social* from Day One. Guilds and other professional organizations emerged to give trades a sense of identity and, in many cases, establish standards that would be communicated to consumers. Membership in a guild was sometimes couched in mystic terms, which evidences how seriously members took their activities. The reputation of a guild was advertising in some limited sense, in that it could include a promise of deliverables to which members were held accountable. But advertising didn't get started as an avocation until printing gave it both shape and purpose, particularly news sheets about halfway through the Second Millennium.

Printed media allowed sellers to post notices of their offerings. Early newspapers in London and the colonies had "advertiser" in their names, and the fees for such placements helped fund them. Limitations of printing technology restricted those early ads to text only, and its interesting how less flamboyant the selling content became when it was no longer spoken but etched in a trackable record. They noted availability and relied on pretty straightforward descriptions of function and purpose. Ads were *searchable*, and since the cost/space devoted to them required brevity there was less opportunity as well as incentive to make grandiose, insupportable claims. That's not to say that early advertising was consistently accurate or fair (and there were no ways to enforce such standards, other than the existing social mechanisms upon which shoppers had relied for centuries). But it was a vast improvement and difference over live-only selling promises made by strangers who might disappear after making a sale.

Print advertising had many of the same effects on commerce that printing had on culture overall. It divorced the content of conversation from the real-time immediacy of listening, thereby buying readers the time and space to consider what they'd been presented. It created an overlay of order on how and where things were sold, as newspaper *classifieds* were ads grouped together by topic or time. In fact, classifieds were effectively conversational media, since readers would "respond" to the offer(s) by comparing and contrasting offers and then referencing past promises. As newspapers grew up, the space available to ads expanded, which allowed sellers to make lengthier arguments. If you wanted to lie, you were going to have to pay for the privilege, though, and you wouldn't probably get away with it many times thereafter. A *reasoned argument* could be dissected, checked, and answered, and it's what people expected.

Print advertising legitimized commerce and became a platform for better, more sustainable communication between buyers and sellers. Ads helped establish trust and that respectability built trust that had been so lacking in the marketplace since the days of Rome.

They were tools for truth, and they empowered us.

EMOTIONS

Media have always been an effort to recreate and share what we sense in the world around us. The more real those expressions, the more authentic and impactful they seem to us. The technology behind media has therefore trended toward an ever-greater ability to render reality, even in service of imagination and artistic vision. You can see that effort in the animals drawn in crude strokes of charcoal on cave walls from before history was recorded, all the way to the 3D high-definition movies we watch today. We've always tried to capture and recreate exactly what we see and hear.

It's apparent in the evolution of photography when you contrast fuzzy, stilted Daguerrotypes with better film, video, and then the clarity of digital files. Sound reproduction went from tinny scratches on rotating cylinders to giant horns attached to styli tracing groves in acetate records, then to rearranged particles on various tape formats to, again, digital files that are indistinguishable from the source material. Even when communicators or artists have chosen to purposefully express things in unreal ways (abstract painting, or ambient soundscapes), they are empowered by the same technologies that allow for the exact rendering of reality.

As media get more "real," they're better at suggesting or referencing emotion. Audiences are shocked by every improvement in this regard. A wax cylinder recording of poet Alfred Lord Tennyson reading lines from his Charge of the Light Brigade must have been a revelation to those people who first heard his voice. Photographs of American Civil War dead shocked the nation, and the first movie of an approaching train engine sent spectators running away from the screen in fear for their lives. Radio, television, and now the Internet are all media that prompt emotion by capturing it in an ever-improving process of reproductive realism. This means media technologies also trend toward improved ability to immerse us in the immediacy of mediated experience. A medieval painting can be moving, but a 3D high-def movie is all-embracing. Listening to a 78 rpm record of Benny Goodman's jazz band is enjoyable, but it doesn't grab you by the collar like a lossless digital recording of a symphony or even pop music favorite. Media have been moving from a tool to reference reality, to being a tool to recreate it that sometimes even surpasses it.

Print has always resisted this trend, or at least existed in parallel to it. Since it was conceived as a code for capturing, translating, and sharing reality, it has stayed basically unchanged over the centuries, even as technologies changed. The technology for printing has constantly improved -- it got faster, for sure -- but the code of text itself is still a code. The Latin alphabet is all but identical to the way it was written 2,000 years ago. Hand presses were replaced by hot type set in metal, then steam-powered presses, but print itself remains print. Reading has stayed the same, too. You had to read a paragraph of text in the 1850s to understand what the author was saying the same way you would have had to read a paragraph two centuries earlier. A book was still a book even if it was produced faster, sold for less, and shared across a wider and deeper community of readers. More words were added to the dictionary, so we could do a better, more nuanced job of describing reality. But text, and thus the words it shared, hasn't changed, and in this unchangingness is its strength.

While pictures and recordings got better eliciting visceral reactions, reading still required time and focus, and thereby continued to deliver arguments the way it always did. The only real area available for improvement was (and still is) the quality of ideas that words communicate. Since words describe reality vs. emerge from it, requiring readers to stand back -- pause, really -- to understand what has been written, they didn't get better at eliciting emotions over time. Individual letter have no emotional quotient. Since the technology for printing also stayed somewhat if not very restrictive of visual representation over time, it helped preserve print's purview as a stand-alone, mostly unchanging communications medium. We saw line drawings in news and advertising in the early 19th century, but it couldn't compete with the words. Its ideas really didn't have to. Mass media were print (i.e. text) media.

Things started to change in the 20th century, as major advances in printing technology allowed for the reproduction of pictures in at least four colors, bringing a new level of realism to what had once been more of a representative accompaniment to text. Pictures really could stand on their own, and there emerged magazines like Life (late 1800s) and Look (mid-1930s) that highlighted visuals over text. Production speeds also increased, as did distribution services, making it much more likely that more people could see the pictures in magazines, which included national newsweeklies that still depended on text, such as Time and the now-defunct Newsweek. Television came about mid-century and started its inexorable rise in popularity and use. Advertising changed accordingly, since using the broad, visceral emotive powers of image were now available to it. Finally, visual imagery could be shared via printed or electronic media that rivaled the imagery prior generations had encountered in their real, daily lives. By the 1950s, stunning visuals could stand-in for textual arguments in newspapers and magazines. Ads were no longer required to state a case as much as present an image of a desired state.

Those ad images were very effective as prompts for conditioned responses, as if the viewer were engaged with the real thing. Seeing a well-off character in an ad would trigger emotions in somewhat predictable ways, not unlike the way encountering royalty or a religious structure did a millennia earlier. *Ad imagery became canned reality*, not necessarily an expression of it in any organic sense but wholly contrived *about* it.

By the second half of the 20th century, imagery was as flexible as a drawer of movable type. Compelling images could be presented to accomplish almost anything. Human beings were already genetically programmed to respond to them, and eons of life experience had taught successive generations that visuals were easier, faster, and more immediately actionable than even a single sentence of text. The emotive power of imagery found a new renaissance (not to be confused with the *old* Renaissance, when it gave way to the power of written, reasoned argument)

Advertising changed in the 1950s, and would continue in a sustained move away from a reliance on words and text. Our communications overall would migrate back toward the broad symbolism that framed and defined our lives in the world prior to Gutenberg's invention.

We'd willingly trade-in our rational text for visual emotions.

PART FOUR:
THE GREAT DISCONNECT

DREAMS

It's difficult to understand media in a vacuum, separate from the context of its experience, whether technological, economic, political, or cultural. Media content originates in those contexts, which then influences the ways it's experienced and interpreted. The ancient Egyptians wrote The Book of the Dead because of their civilization's obsession with the afterlife. Martin Luther's bestseller was enabled by new printing technology, but its revolutionary and timely theses drove purchases. Mathew Brady's use of quicker photo capture tech made it possible to snap shots of Civil War dead strewn across still-smoking battlefields, but feelings about the war affected their interpretation. Media and content are inseparable. I'm particularly interested in how those contextual influences impact both what and how content has been shared over time, particularly in relation to the balance between words and images.

By the 1950s, the century's progress in enabling print media technology to render imagery in color and clarity had reached new heights, as had the reproduction and distribution tools necessary to quite literally put that content into the hands of a true "mass market" of consumers, making it easier and more viscerally impactful to communicate in pictures, sometimes in lieu of text altogether. Picture magazines were all the rage, even though they'd been around for decades. Televisions found their way into more and more peoples' homes, providing moving pictures to a population that had formerly made due with static images. Visual communication allowed for more blunt and emotional communication, evidencing the cliche that **a picture is worth a thousand words**.

This shift was no more apparent than in commercial conversations -- advertising -- as marketers exploited the use of images and symbols to promote products for which they once would have had to argue in words. There's good reason why we associate this decade with very explicit, visual guides to standardized norms for beauty, success, and happiness. Ads established and then propagated those symbols more effectively in the 1950s than ever before.

It wasn't just happenstance, either. Just as the technology of media allowed for ever-better rendering of reality that made the symbolism it communicated more effective, the broader commercial context needed it to do so. It needed advertising to transcend *reality* and sell more *dreams*.

America had a vast amount of industrial capacity to manufacture the armaments that helped it and its allies win WWII. It also avoided any sustained damage to its infrastructure, the attack on Pearl Harbor notwithstanding. This created a two-part challenge once the war ended: the factories needed to keep their workers employed, as well as offer jobs to returning soldiers and, second, in order to keep running, they'd have to manufacture things other than bullets and guns. Much of this industrial capacity could be put to use helping rebuild the countries that hadn't escaped the horrible destruction of the war. But it was only part of the equation. The home market needed to be served, just as a war-weary generation of consumers needed to be satisfied. The only question was with *what?*

Advertising during the first half of the century had worked fairly similarly to the ways it had succeeded for centuries prior. It was primarily a tool for transferring information, admittedly imperfectly. But its reliance of words and printed text had grounded advertisers in some accountability and responsibility for what they promised, just as the medium of print advertising had required them to make their cases in words and reasoned arguments. Further, the economic status of many Americans had been just above subsistence, again not altogether different than the way their grandparents had lived, and the technical innovations at the beginning of the 20th century offered them bold, functional improvements, like electric lights, telephones, vacuum cleaners, and washing machines. Even baked bread and fresh eggs sold on grocery shelves instead of made at home was a big deal. Advertising had informed and inspired consumers with these true innovations. Selling things that were demonstrably better than the things they hoped to replace must have been a marketers' dream!

America was different at the start of the second half of the century was different. The economy had never been stronger. More people were more affluent than every before. The *zeitgeist* of the culture was confident and empowered. Though there was all of that industrial capacity that couldn't be allowed to go fallow, the bold leaps in product innovation -- mostly replacing manual actions with electrified or automated ones -- had already been made. Telling people that a blender could replace manual mixing was no longer news; worse, many people already possessed one. No amount of argued text could change these facts.

The solution? It was time to build new consumer dreams, and transform advertising from communicating based on argued *needs* to creating fantasies of imagined *wants*.

Using the the tools of media creation and distribution to deliver the emotional triggers always associated with blunt symbolism was an obvious way to deliver that solution. As applied to advertising, the 1950s saw visuals shift from being the supportive content in ads, to become the entire pitch. What ads endeavored to sell wasn't a reasoned improvement over known needs any longer, but rather propagate creative differences between otherwise similar choices. The challenge was no longer to sell the merits of a vacuum cleaner; instead, ads had to invent associative or emotional differences between one of a number of purchase *options*. There's always been an aspirational component of advertising, since there's one behind every commercial transaction, but now it was the sole purpose of the activity.

Factories no longer made different products as much as similar ones that would be differentiated by cosmetic variation, which would be then imagined by the visual symbols of advertising. American industrial capacity needed to keep churning, requiring each year that marketers find new ways to promote what was effectively the same stuff. It was easier to make these cases in visuals and symbols, immersing consumers in moments of media experience that evoked blunt and immediate emotional responses, than it was to explain things to them in linear arguments that could be challenged or rejected.

As words gave ground to imagery, the communications business shifted from reality to dreams. It was wildly successful.

OGILVY

Words weren't wholly replaced by imagery in 1950s advertising (or in news reporting overall). It would take decades for the trend to mature and change the very purposes of public communication. Advertising had a patron saint of words during the early days of this transition named David Ogilvy. Ogilvy literally wrote the book (a few, in fact) on how to make reasoned arguments that would sell. Inadvertently, he commemorated the fading utility of words and reasoned arguments in advertising.

His 1958 ad for Rolls-Royce is an illustrative example of his approach to advertising. The headline read "At 60 miles an hour the loudest noise in this new Rolls-Royce comes from the electric clock," followed by a numbered list of 19 reasons why the design and manufacture of the clock and other functional components proved the company's expertise, and therefore the inherent value of its products. A visual of a Rolls-Royce accompanied most versions of the list, usually portraying the vehicle in an everyday suburban setting. This was a shorthand way of helping readers imagine driving the exotically expensive cars to pick up dry cleaning, or get kids from school.

Could an image alone have sold the car without the text? I wonder, but I doubt it. Buying a Rolls-Royce was an even bigger conceptual and financial leap than it is today. Its visual symbolism, however well-known, would have appeared out of reach to most consumers. The only way to bridge that distance was through a well-articulated argument, if crossing that distance was possible at all.

Ogilvy's ads for Hathaway shirts in 1951 are another example of the utility of words in advertising, this time in service of a less-expensive product. The language is dated now, promising stitching that "has an ante-bellum elegance about it" on shirts that will give "quiet satisfaction" because they're done in "such impeccable taste." But the ad made a cogent case for buying the shirts, supported with an image intended to telegraph style and attitude. The tone and phrasing was conversational, the words more simple than complex, befitting the ideas they conveyed. Ogilvy's arguments seemed always grounded in functional, demonstrable reality. They were intended to communicate those truths in the most compelling way possible.

He was not a trained writer. In fact, Ogilvy had been a history major at England's Oxford University but never graduated, choosing to work instead as an apprentice chef at a hotel in Paris, and then as a door-to-door salesman for a cooking supply company. He penned his company's sales instruction manual, which was celebrated by <u>Fortune</u> magazine 30 years later as the best sales manual ever written. Ogilvy was a product of his times; the early part of the 20th century, just like many centuries before it, greatly valued the ability to write and a willingness to read. Words were tools of empowerment and success, which supported arguments for mobility and change. They were used to destroy existing or assumed symbols of authority or power in order to accomplish that change.

Advertising had consisted of such content since its inception, with varying degrees of detail, honesty, and efficacy. Overall, that content had been dictated in many ways by print technology's inability to render realistic imagery. Ads had to use text to make cases for ideas and emotions, which is what the code of words does best, if not only. Ogilvy was not only a guardian of this practice, but perhaps its most accomplished practitioner.

I believe written commercial communication, just like the commerce underlying it, was experienced as a *conversation*. Thought it's fashionable today to reference advertising in the 50s & 60s as "one way," using words is inherently "two-way" by the very experiences of reading: writers *talk* to us, as we *talk back* when we read. We reference this fact in the vernacular when we say that a writer "*said* this or that." The cognitive process of reading requires us to engage with the content of what's being communicated, not simply react to its form. Words are analyzed and either embraced, rejected, or ignored, while visual stimuli are experienced through immediate reaction. The only mechanism of conversation that consumers of print advertising lacked was a specific external tool *to talk back*, at least directly. People could comment indirectly through communication with friends and, of course, through buying the advertised product or service (or not).

Advertising was *social,* albeit imperfectly, and ads -- just as words overall, upon which they were based -- literally *talked* to us, just as we talked back. When ads moved to rely on visuals and broad-brush strokes of emotional imagery, those conversations stopped.

In 1960, Ogilvy published a treatise entitled "How to create advertising that sells." Typical for him, it was organized into a list, this time 38 entries that laid out the case for effective commercial conversation. It was a *textual infographi*c on the merits of words over symbol and image, except for the nascent medium of TV (where he argued that the rules for written content still applied, but should be rendered in units parsed appropriately for a visual medium). His tenets were strikingly simple and sincere: be truthful, simple, declarative, real, avoid creative distractions. The outline itself embodied those rules as it presented each bulleted point. It argued for conversation over assertion, words over images.

Many of his words were already going unread or unheard by the time Ogilvy shared them with the world, however. His agency would be wildly successful, but it would grow and morph as the 60s and 70s progressed, shifting ever-greater amounts of its effort away from text-based conversation toward the presentation of symbolic imagery. The ideas that were embedded as part of the form and function of that traditional commercial communication would give way to the older truths of the visceral power of pictures.

An advertising revolution had begun, and it would spell the end of advertising as a word-driven medium for communicating truth.

CREATIVE

As I suggested a few chapters ago, commerce in post-WWII America was all about keeping the country's immense manufacturing capacity occupied. Functional innovation couldn't come up with frequent enough improvements, thereby necessitating the marketing of associative and emotional differences between otherwise similar products and services. This required a new way of selling things. Reasoned arguments couldn't be used to make the case for minor, cosmetic differences. Fortunately, advances in media production and distribution technology meant that advertisers could rely more on the blunt, low-information impact of imagery than on the textual, reasoned arguments upon which they'd relied traditionally. The approach produced unimagined economic success and lasting, bold symbols: the period gave us "the perfect family" in marketing -- two kids, two cars, suburban tract house in which the wife served while the husband went off to work -- as well as in the creative content of TV programming.

It also bred a new generation of consumers who were all too familiar with the promises those symbols communicated, and grew to become deeply suspicious of them.

The post-war generation had been trained since they were little kids to know what the images meant. The problem was that much of their experience didn't substantiate the promises of those broad symbols. As they grew up, they weren't *happier* because of the way they dressed, or *more satisfied* with their lives because of the soda pop they consumed. You could say that by the time the 1960s were underway, *the conversation* the public had with institutions of power, whether commercial or political, was not only no longer substantive, but it wasn't believable. Advertising had defaulted to symbolism to sell, and it started coming back to haunt the brands and institutions that had embraced the approach.

The disconnect between what had been promised, whether overtly or implicitly, and what got delivered amounted to *a lie*.

It wasn't a black and white situation. The advertising practices devised (or reinvented) in the 50s still worked, of course; a funny or surprising ad was still entertaining, and segments of the buying public were willing to make purchasing decisions thereupon, especially among older demographics. Symbols worked. Coke attached world peace to its pitch through a spot in which hippy-types sang "I'd like to teach the world to sing in perfect harmony." 3M's Scotch Tape promised to make Halloween happier. Celebrities sold themselves in the service of a wide variety of products, from Paula Prentiss and Jim Hutton swathing themselves in Coppertone sun lotion, to Sammy Davis wearing a Nehru suit.

But overall, and especially in communication intended for younger consumers, ads got racier, more self-depreciating, and ironic, often times evidencing an almost conscious distancing from the idea that they needed to sell a symbolic image, let alone make or prove a case. The "new" thinking was to sell something by actively trying *not to sell anything*. For instance, William Bernbach's DDBO created ads for the Volkswagen Beetle started with headlines like "Ugly" and "Lemon." They were wildly popular and, because the cars were cheap and looked so unlike any other vehicles on the road, sales rose with consumers interested in making a counter-cultural statement. Though the ads featured witty copy, the images of the Bug underneath the headlines literally said it all. They made a *no-sale sell.*

These practices were labelled *The Creative Revolution* and would not only last well into the 1960s and 1970s, but continue to dictate how advertising sees its purpose and approaches today, whether via ads or the latest social media campaigns.

It would further destroy the authority of brands and the institutions they served.

The destruction would take time because it had been long in the making. There'd always been a tension in advertising between the uses of words and images. Since the early 20th century. one school believed that advertising should explain in detail why a product or service was worth buying, as if it were the one-on-one pitch of a salesman, only writ for a mass audience. Advertising executives like Albert Lasker, John E. Kennedy and Claude Hopkins were major promoters of this approach. The other camp believed that visuals and "big" creative ideas were the way to go. People like Raymond Rubicam, Leo Burnett, and Bill Bernbach tended to approach words as if they were "word pictures," not long arguments -- low information but high impact, like an image -- and wrote amazingly memorably emotive slogans, tag lines, and jingles. Many of the later proponents of this approach were outright art directors, not writers. David Ogilvy, a bit of an iconoclast, had feet in both camps, but his bias was toward words and reasoned argument.

It became clear as the 60s progressed that the winners of the Creative Revolution were the visual camp, as they provided a faster and more immediate path to overcome consumers' distrust of what they were tasked to promote. But they didn't do it by offering a counter-argument for that hesitation; rather, they simply worked around and past it, replacing sales pitches with the inspiration of emotional ideas as the driver of consumer choice. In the 1950s, branded communication had given up its self-anointed responsibility to argue and inform through words. A decade later, they no longer felt obligated to inform or earn trust, and instead embraced a mandate simply to *entertain*. Entertainment meant even more *announcement* than *conversation*, less *debate* and more *declaration*. Ads themselves became works of art, celebrated for their ability to capture and express emotions. Advertising executives were honored for their ability to craft memorable lines, not forge lasting relationships based on sales. It became possible for ads to be great even if the products or services that paid for them were less so.

This shift was made all the more effective by the nascent growth of consumer research which also came onto the scene in the 1960s. Research tools like surveys, focus groups, and psychological profiling gave advertisers greater and deeper insight into the minds and motivations of buyers. Armed with this better understanding of what consumers wanted and cared about, they could have decided to craft better, more compelling arguments to reaffirm and substantiate their brand messages.

Instead, The Creative Revolution taught marketers to tell consumers what they wanted to hear and see. The disconnect between commercial speech and its ability to share truth was complete.

It's like we went back to sleep.

COOL

Marshall McLuhan was a media theorist who studied and wrote about the ways people interact with technology in the 1950s and 1960s. His models for "hot" and "cool" media and the social role of printing were groundbreaking (he had a particular fascination with movable type, as do I). The language he used to express his ideas was often convoluted, often on purpose, so many of his contemporaries either didn't understand him or didn't try. I find his thinking illustrative of both the power and role of words, and his analyses of technology compelling, though incomplete.

I remember reading his first book while I was a freshman in high school; The Mechanical Bride had been published more than two decades earlier, in 1951, and analyzed a variety of visuals (mostly ads). McLuhan was interested in the symbolism of advertising content and the ways our sense of sight affected what we perceived. He believed that the act of perception was as important to our conclusions as was the content of what we saw. It blew me away, and I quickly hit my local library to find something else by him. The only other title they had was Understanding Media, which he'd published in 1964. I devoured it too fast to grasp everything he said.

But I could tell that his theories about "hot" and "cool" media were huge. "Hot" media were those that focused on one sense, contained a high amount of information, and required the perceiver to do little other than consume it. "Cool" media were multi-sensory, had low amounts of information, and therefore needed the participation of perceivers in order to complete it. So reading text was hot media, but watching someone speak to you was cool. Images were hot because they utilized only one sense, but watching a video with sound was cool. Radio was cool, which I still don't understand. The reason his distinctions mattered was because he believed media effect culture by their very form, not the content they communicate. His beliefs were summed up in his famous slogan "the medium is the message."

Looking at our interaction with technology and its impact on our perception as a lens through which to understand how we communicate is very relevant today. It helps explain what happens when we migrate content from one medium to another (i.e. why a visual joke doesn't work as an audio file, or a TV spot needs to be adapted to social media instead of just stuffing it into a player). But it only goes so far. Consider this: you read text, then look at a picture. Both actions involve your sense of sight. McLuhan would classify them as similar experiences because both media are single-sense and therefore "hot." Yet the substance of those perceptions -- reading the code of words vs. experiencing the moment of image -- is very different. The differences extend to the experience immediately prior and following them, and the *contexts* within which those perceptions take place.

I'd offer that instead of looking for meaning in the sense or senses a particular media technology engages, we should consider the type and amount of code contained in the communication itself. Sensory stimuli, especially sight, are low code/immediate reaction communications tools, while words/text are high code/ delayed reaction. Being agnostic to these foundational qualities of content experience leaves us without an understanding of the possible outcomes of that engagement. Content matters.

So when McLuhan wrote in the <u>Gutenberg Galaxy</u> that print had made possible most of the intellectual and social movements of history, he was really describing the facility of written code to communicate meaning and accomplish understanding. When he posited that video enabled a more tribal, "cool" engagement with content that would create *a global village*, he was right to describe it as a move away from our reliance on the phonetic alphabet to a more immediate, visceral involvement. What he missed was that the content of that media was more like the blunt, authoritarian content of sensory experience prior to printed words/text. He called it *tribal* but didn't explore what it meant, preferring instead to warn us that we needed to be aware of its implications, whatever they were.

Details aside, however, McLuhan saw the changes in the balance between text and imagery in our media that had been occurring since a century before he was born. He described the shift from distillation and considered response provided by words rendered as text, to the participatory, real-time experience provided by imagery. He focused on the technologies that enabled that media consumption -- he was a media theorist, after all -- and not on the content prior to its communication, or the conclusions after the electronic devices had been turned off.

He also blew up words, admitting that he sometimes did so purposely, making comments that were impossible to decipher. It could have been a result of his desire to make people think, or an outcome of a deviously playful nature. Perhaps it was a combination of both, but he'd regularly refuse to explain the meaning of the phrase "the medium is the message," choosing instead to challenge people to define it. He also mashed up his own writing, publishing a book in 1967 entitled <u>The Medium is the Massage</u> and attributing it to a typographical error in the book proof that he elected to leave unchanged. Or not.

In doing so, he reaffirmed my belief that words matter, not because of their technology of reproduction but because of the experiences and understanding they enable. McLuhan believed that all technologies communications communicated meaning by their very use, having written that light bulbs were a communications medium that enabled community because they lit an area. I'm not sure I agree with that idea either, but his insights were profoundly important to our understanding of the change underway in our society, whether evidenced in how commercial speech was created and experienced, or by the ways news programming was packaged and disseminated.

Ultimately, I think it just turned out that *the message really is the message.* This is particularly relevant when the advertising or other media content purposefully contains no real message at all.

PART FIVE:
FINDING OURSELVES
IN THE 21ST CENTURY

MOBILE

Human beings are more physically mobile today than in any other time in our history. Whether movement to and from activities during any given day, to the more broad geographic life-direction moves that many of us have made in our pasts or will in our futures, we are free to move about all the time. We're rarely in the same place for long. A variety of technologies and businesses exist to get us from one place to another, and we have reasons both commercial and recreational to use them. Entire mythologies celebrate *the open road* and the freedom that comes with owning a car or motorcycle. We hope to *get away* on airplanes from the routines that dampen our souls, and then we're rewarded for the miles we've traveled. Though slowing probably due to recent economic conditions, three-fourths of Americans drive to work each day, and spend almost a half hour traveling in each direction. Most of us will move to a new community at least once in our lives. Six in ten will die in place different and perhaps distant from where they were born.

It wasn't always like this. Before the Industrial Revolution, there were no good ways to get about, and certainly no way of doing so. A horse could walk three miles per hour and trot seven. Travel by ship was accomplished at the whim of the winds, and wasn't priced within reach of most folks. Peasants lived where their families had lived before them, tending to nearby fields or businesses until they could pass them onto their own children. They relied on their own two feet as their primary means of movement. Economics didn't favor travel or relocation (though the Black Death necessitated that peasants travel to find the best wages). They also had no political authority to move about; many medieval *villeins* worked as indentured servants who needed to ask for their lords' favor before they went someplace. People didn't travel much, far, or particularly fast, so it's no surprise that moving about was also considered bad form. Communities were suspicious of strangers. Vagabonds, gypsies, and other inveterate travelers were culturally suspect.

There's some evidence that individuals and families were *socially mobile* through most of the second millennium of the Common Era...much more so than we are. Studies of family names in English society suggest that there were no permanent "rich" or "poor," but that people moved quickly through these class distinctions (in both directions). For every peasant who trod a field just as his parents did, another one learned a trade or brought a skill to a nearby village and amassed more wealth than had the prior generation. The causes of this fluidity and ease of social movement are not certain, but it puts to shame the reality of social mobility in America today. While we physically move about with relative ease and frequency, it's far more likely that our grandchildren will circulate in the same social and economic communities as we do. We Americans are presented with fewer opportunities for class movement in our own lives, despite all the propaganda suggesting otherwise.

We all equally own the dream of social mobility, even if it's not reality. I find it interesting that while we move about physically, our hearts and minds live in closed villages that we take with us.

Our mobile tech gives us portable tools for the experiences of community that our ancestors relied upon. We move about, but we're always embedded in our collections of friends, associates, and interests, allowing us the simulacra of mobility when our minds and hearts really pretty much stay put.

We have less incentive as well as less opportunity to leave those various communities we carry with us. When the infrequent medieval peasants had the fortitude to travel a good distance from his or her birthplace, they had to overcome a distance that meant separation, usually permanent. Once relocated, they were no longer a part of the social or economic structure in which they'd formerly lived. They were disconnected. Conversely, we are on the move, but we're always connected socially, always grounded and affirmed by our communities. Staying associated costs nothing except charges to our time. *Stationary* minds come with the new physical *mobility*.

We have much more in common with our medieval ancestors who stayed put than we think. *Community* is the killer app of mobile tech, not any particular brand name technology platform.

This has immense implications for the ways businesses, institutions, and people communicate.

First, today's mobility affords **just-in-time knowledge**. Untethered from desks and even geographic places in general, consumers no longer have to possess preconceived notions or information in preparation for making some future decision. The smartphone in their hands allows them to access knowledge at the exact point at which they require it, from choosing a restaurant, pricing a product, looking for an airfare, buying or selling stock, to even picking a political candidate. Mobile communications has nothing to do with entertainment or something as generically inert as "content." It's less *image*, more *action*, usually inspired with words.

Second, much of this knowledge -- especially its vetting and endorsement -- doesn't and won't come from old authorities (think institutions we have abandoned and no longer "visit," virtually or in the flesh) and instead from the communities that travel with us. **Authority is outsourced** to the peer-to-peer networks that we carry with us in our pockets. We trust and rely on them and our conversations with them, and not on the symbolic declarations of brands and other old-fashioned authorities we left behind, even though now they chase us with pretty videos and other nonsense.

Third, just like a benefit of living in a small village was that people knew what they did, where they *fit*, and what they would/could do, the proof of mobile community utility is not in how it provides experiences of brands or other institutions, but rather **how it enables community members to get things done**. It's about providing the data necessary for the knowledge people need to enable just-in-time experience they want.

This mobile reality requires a language or code to use in order to create and share this information. That code is words, and its delivery medium text. Only words provide the depth, detail, and repeatability to realize the potential of our mobile tech. So while marketers still talk in the broad emotive and symbolic terms they inherited from the mid-20th century -- even wrapped in creative uses of new digital media -- the power of peer-to-peer conversations is reasserting itself, whether or not they grasp it. Communities aren't *of* or *with* brands, but rather they might talk *about* them. The brands themselves are artifacts of the static, outdated visual symbolism of a bygone era.

Words are the tools that allows us to thrive in our communities, wherever they...or we...might be.

SILENCE

The world is very noisy, especially its cities, and it has been that way for centuries. Romans complained of the cacophony on their streets two thousand years ago. By the time the Industrial Revolution gave us factories and began to spin-off devices that ran, coughed, or otherwise chugged along on evermore crowded city streets, the sounds only increased in number and volume. Wagons and horses still clacked along cobblestone streets. Crates were loaded and unloaded. Whistles and horns were blown to do everything from direct traffic, to announce that peddlers had everything from toys to, well, horns to sell.

The sounds of people were everywhere. Garbage scavengers called to one another as they did their work in the dead of night, and then chimney sweeps announced themselves to their masters just before dawn. Salesmen and women announced their wares standing outside of their shops or in front of their carts in open markets. People talked, laughed, and yelled. When London passed its first anti-noise campaign in the 1860s, it wasn't in reaction to the sounds of machinery but rather an effort to quiet street musicians.

There has traditionally been little to no escape from noise, especially during the summer months, since people had to leave their windows open in hopes of staying cool. The sounds of marketplaces were unavoidable year-round, as were crowds when you simply needed to get somewhere. The only way to avoid noise was to be rich enough to be among the very few who could build homes far away from it. Even then, though, the noises of everyday life were never silenced completely.

What is noise? It's an every-day descriptive for sounds that are unwanted or bothersome. A noise is a sound you don't want or choose to hear. So it's not that the individual sounds of life are inherently noisy; sales announcements, the cries of guild members to one another, or the unconscious bleats from machinery on those medieval or Industrial Era-streets weren't necessarily individually bothersome. But taken together, they made for noise, above which people had to listen in order to hear and be heard. You'd imagine that the challenge presented by this environment wasn't to try and simultaneously hear all of the sounds, or speak to them, but rather identify a single sought-after sound, or find a listener who could hear what you wanted to say. Successful communication in noisy cities wasn't a result of multi-tasking but rather *mono-tasking*...filtering out the noise that didn't matter, so you could focus on the stuff that did, usually one at a time.

In science and technology, content that is too jumbled to be of any use (or reveals no obvious pattern) is called *noise*. It's the distortion you hear when you turn up a speaker too loud, or when your Internet connection makes your VOIP call echo. Noise is what researchers encounter when incidental or unrelated data corrupt an experiment. In physics, you could call noise the lack of order in any medium, so it's a synonym for less structure and more entropy. In music, noise occurs when tones violate their harmonics, yielding sounds that are off-key or, when played together, just sound *wrong* (there's a value judgment therein, though, as the debut of Stravinsky's

Rite of Spring in 1913 was considered so dissonant that it cause a riot. It's now a classic).

If you think more broadly about data, noise isn't just aural; it can be visual, olfactory or, for that matter, tactile. Just imagine the cacophony of sights and smells on those 18th or 19th century streets. The variety of things you'd touch or bump into, even the very grit in the air you breathed, would have made the experience *feel and taste noisy*. People have endured multiple, concurrent, noisy demands for their attention for centuries.

Maybe that's why we've always valued *silence*.

Every world religion has taught that silence is key to enlightened understanding of self and the cosmos. Monks have taken vows to never utter a word. Mahatma Gandhi wrote "In the attitude of silence the soul finds the path in a clearer light, and what is elusive and deceptive resolves itself into crystal clearness." We use a moment of silence in public ceremonies to honor things that matter to us, and equate keeping silent with not just respect and thoughtfulness but, as Socrates wrote about constructive collaboration, "If we who does not know kept silent, discord would cease." When we want a moment to consider something, we say "gimme a minute," which usually involves a minute of avoiding other sensory inputs.

I'd offer that s*ilence* can be considered a synonym for *focus,* and with focus comes the depth and accuracy of perception and truthfulness of conclusions that those quotations from philosophers affirm. It's also a word for *pause*, or *reflection* which can be applied to any or all of the five senses. We have always valued the outcomes of those moments of quiet and calm far more than we've ever valued quick decisions. Judgments made impatiently used to be called *snap* or *knee-jerk*, and they were suspect simply due to the speed by which they were reached.

The communications media of past generations required such pauses mostly due to their inherent qualities or limitations, even as recently as late last century. Postal mail service forced writers to wait days for a reply. Phone calls often went unanswered and, when voicemail machines came onto the scene, callers could leave a message but still had to wait an undetermined time for a reply. Advertising was broadcast, literally, which meant messages were thrown out at people, and then marketers had to wait days or weeks to see evidence of their efficacy. News events were sometimes slow to be shared, especially globally. The questions that anybody wanted to ask, whether for a school or work project, or personal interest, couldn't be answered by simply entering a search query into a computer terminal, but required sometimes arduous research in a public library (which meant traveling to a facility, thumbing through card catalogues, finding books, and then reading them).

Reading itself is a *forced pause*. It empowers individuals the way that the cacophony of noise around them denies them that control: reading can be "turned on or off" based on your choice; readers control the speed at which the information is presented, and can choose to accentuate (i.e. turn up the volume) on a passage by rereading or contemplating it; and reading blocks out other forms of sensory input because it requires focus. It is the ultimate mono-task.

But we no longer need to read, focus, or pause to understand our world, do we? While all of history has been a battle to avoid or ignore the noise around us, we now encourage engagement with it. There's an entire theology to support the benefits of multi-tasking and speed/frequency of engagement. Brief is better, vague is easier, and incomplete is somehow more authentic than detailed, specific, and whole.

Silence is no longer a necessary or aspirational good as much as it's an anachronistic, limiting idea. We choose instead to simultaneously engage with watching videos, sending short bursts of text to one another, perhaps listening to music, and doing other things as much as our fingers and attention spans can accomplish.

But it's still noise.

BRIEF

TED was founded in 1984 as a conference about technology, entertainment, and design. It has since grown into a thriving global operation, offering multiple events on every subject imaginable, a robust online menu of videos, and various programs to get people involved in creating and/or consuming the stuff they host. TED's tagline -- Ideas worth spreading -- is supported by its approach to the content its participants enjoy. If a presentation isn't shorter than 18 minutes, it's not worth enduring.

This embrace of brevity has freed innumerable people to tee-up content (for which they're not paid, by the way) and many more to attend their events (for which they *do* pay). And it underlies the pitch TED makes to its participants when it calls itself "a community welcoming people from every discipline and culture who seek a deeper understanding of the world." The reality is that its offering is less deep than broad, and participants don't have to really work, study, or take time to understand any particular subject. All it takes is witnessing an 18-minute presentation to be engaged in the world.

It's pure genius.

Now, 18 minutes of information on a topic that you might not otherwise have ever considered is a good thing, and there's no way such exposure can't have at least some benefit to your worldview thereafter. There's nothing wrong with it; rather, the TED approach is emblematic of our deification of *brief,* which does involve pretty significant trade-offs in our lives.

Brief used to be synonymous with *incomplete* or *ill-informed.* Pretty much every society prior to ours celebrated not just lengthy exposition, but required some heavy-duty time-consuming qualifications of its content-creators and the audiences given access to them. History was written mostly by specialists, not generalists, and innovation was usually the result of dedicated, long-term trial and error effort (and not the unexpected flash of a dabbler's lightning insight). Cultures valued individuals who made such commitments to their trade or academic topics, and institutions arose to support as well as certify them.

People used to spend a lot of time trying to understand each other, assuming they tried at all. There were no shortcuts; even the tools, like books, were often hard to get, and access to conversation with experts was closely limited to those who had already been pre-approved by their chosen studies or initiated into the club or society that hosted educated discourse. When opened, thoughtful books were a chore to read. Written (and spoken) language was heavy with conventions and rules that made for long sentences filled with various clauses. Reading was a time-consuming affair, as was listening to a speech or lecture, which could last for hours.

This meant that most regular folks were locked out of such conversations. It was elitist, by definition, and in Western Europe such dialogues were restricted almost exclusively to white men. The trade-off was that the arrangement enabled the creation of original content, however imperfectly or unfairly. The sheer weight of its strictures informed debate and prompted development. This structure wasn't at fault as much as it's restrictions were; the explicit limits on quality and content were sensible, while the implicit barriers based on gender and class were not.

Now, services like TED and online conversation in general require no such pre-qualification or commitment for participation. Anybody can be an expert on anything, whether presenter or audience member, since everyone is empowered to have an opinion. Everything imaginable, by dint of have been translated from vague thought or reaction to a brief comment or tweet, is deserving of an audience and then propagation into the mediasphere. If we're exposed to something *we somehow know it*, and then we can challenge any or every component of the content. I think this is why, for instance, there's such a thriving community of global climate change deniers; there's enough stuff available online that people with no education in science, climate, or analytic methodologies can consume and, thereby, be experts, too, if only for a moment. The fact that the vast majority of scientists agree on a conclusion means nothing. Any and every idea is equally worth spreading, and will be vetted by the popularity contests of Internet search and quippy online comments by the fellow uninitiated.

The same phenomena cripples our political public discourse in America, as many of us have a desire to pass judgments on the vagaries of governance without commensurate ability to understand its complexity. We are "values voters" or have interest in one issue to the exclusion of all others. With the abbreviated formats in which we receive and share our information, we confuse *brevity* with *clarity*. Too many words means inchoate thinking. We prefer blunt, simple, symbolic gestures.

Something similar is going on in most branded communications today, where brief, symbolic gestures like tweets, likes, and viral videos that rival TED's Talk videos for shortness are used as the tools upon which relationships with customers are based. Why should oil companies take the time (and risk) to explain to consumers why they're reasonably not really investing in an alternate energy future that won't come to pass for another century or more, when feel-good TV ads with images of wind farms and actors saying we need energy from "all sources" will satisfy viewers who only have a moment of attention to spare? One soap better than another? No, just differently funny or somehow identified in its creative delivery.

Today, we all get to participate, but our involvement is to touch briefly a variety of subjects without really knowing or building upon any of them. It's easier than going to school forever and having peers challenge everything we do down to the use of punctuation in a research paper, but it's nowhere near as valuable. *Knowledge* and *entertainment* are not the same thing, and our brief embrace of *everything* instead of studied engagement with *something* leaves us either unaware or ill-informed or, worse, we risk being manipulated by entities that know how to wield the power of symbol and imagery. Brief is the language of command-and-control communication. Maybe that's why we're all so suspicious and distrusting of most authorities these days, just as our medieval ancestors were of their bakers and cobblers.

Is this circumstance in which we find ourselves better or worse than being encumbered by the historic limitations once put on creating and sharing information? We may have replaced the old elitism based on *substance* with a new elitism based on *process*. The former is imperfect, takes time, and risks failure. The latter is easy, fast, and promises only success. Everyone gets it while only a limited few accessed it before.

I wonder what we'd learn if we quizzed an audience at a TED talk on their understanding of topics, say, a day after enjoying a spate of 18-minute presentations. I'm sure they'd report their satisfaction (you can learn as much on the organization's web page). Imagine if those attendees spent 18 minutes reading something and trying to actually *learn* something themselves.

They might gain a deeper understanding of the world even.

NOW

United Airlines breaks a checked guitar. There are weird goings-on at Taco Bell and Domino's. The Iranians hold a flawed election, and Ashton files for divorce from Demi. Motrin produces a dumb video while Old Spice creates hilarious ones. The cable repair guy falls asleep on the job. Banks are run by a bunch of S.O.B. capitalists. Over past few years, these were among the topics that caused firestorms of passion and frequency on social media platforms...only to be forgotten and then replaced by other firestorms which were promptly forgotten and replaced. The "trend" that mattered most, and still does, is that the half-life of trends can now be measured in nanoseconds.

That's because *they were announcements that water is wet*, telling us little to nothing that we didn't already know, while providing no reason to ponder or otherwise internalize the information. The primary action that recipients took was to forward the news. Today's trends are not so much about *understanding* as they are about *propagating*. Less take-in and more hand-off. Reaction, not cognition.

The most compelling trend today is that trends are compelling, if only immediately and for an instant. There is no real public awareness or capacity to complete anything long-term anymore. Rather, we choose to gaze into a huge mirror and watch ourselves, in the present, like my cat exploring my office for the umpteenth first time.

We are trapped in a constant *now*.

The fact that social platforms are often used to restate the obvious is no surprise. People did it while chatting in Roman baths and meeting at London coffeehouses. Monk scribes wrote exclamation points on the margins of medieval manuscripts, and readers have been writing letters to newspaper editors since the medium was invented. Your parents (or maybe grandparents) might seem like hapless Luddites, but they were once young and clued into the latest topics and technologies. Granted, their "networks" for communicating were often powered by unamplified voices, smudgy type, and TV tubes instead of transistors, but they cared about the important issues of their day. They got involved and shared their opinions and hopes with one another. We have always been social and found ways to chat and *tsk-tsk* with one another about the day's events.

The behaviors are old, but the broader trends that we experience today via our interaction with online media are different. They create a sense of *now* from which we can't seem to escape.

Dispersed tech means that content can get teed-up and accessed from an infinite number of sources, so the volume and frequency is deep and incessant. Content can be reviewed in an instant on selfsame technology devices, which has the capacity to tell us what *others* have just read or viewed and, thereby, encourage us to check the same things. This means that views of a news tidbit can multiply quickly, or get replaced by another news item a moment later. It requires that most online trends be simple and brief, often a picture or a paragraph or two of something that can be consumed in an instant.

We yack like our ancestors did, only more briefly and more often, and we do so based on what others are yacking about. It's wonderfully circular and self-referencing.

What we **do** with out chatting is different, too. We are all horribly busy. I have professional friends who fill their days with back-to-back meetings and don't have time for an unscheduled phone call or bathroom break. For the rest of us who aren't that imprisoned by our diaries, there's still little time to handle that constant stream of trending information that comes at us on our smartphones, tablets and laptops. But we get things presented in bite-sized portions, which we then taste and either delete or forward. Nuance and insight are not qualities often associated with today's trends, but rather are directly and inversely proportional to trending speed of delivery. Our online trends are *simple* and *quick*, and intended for consumption in a moment, not over time.

That's because the breadth and depth of our online trends are intended for online consumption, not applicable to subsequent action or use in the real world. We never used to track trending as a quality with inherent value, though it was obvious to people what topics were being talked about at work on a Monday morning or during world events that had been covered by the limited, mass media. We didn't call them *trends* because, well, they weren't…they were *topics of note*, perhaps, or simply stuff that got mentioned. The moments spent engaged with that stuff wasn't vested with much meaning, if any. Real trends were phenomena that had implications in the real world and usually involved actions, or series of actions, which earned them our attention. Trends had to gather some traction over time (and space) and involve qualities that weren't immediately apparent, which meant that they were often only seen and understood in retrospect.

Getting lots of people to click on a video or link to a starlet's new outfit would have been called a *stunt*, not a trend, because it would have been over before we'd known it even happened.

Believing otherwise is no different than the ways people used to interact with visual stimuli in the days before writing. A brief, vague tweet or snippet of words is more visual data than textual, in that it's usually low and/or incomplete information that elicits an immediate reaction. There's a lot of it, and we have little time to consider what we see -- *it's noisy* -- so that our reactions are often to quickly classify the content *funny*, *stupid*, *save*, *share*, and then take that next action. We want to get it off our radar and move onto the next trigger for our attention. Each interaction is discreet, even if we track topics from moment to moment. Without the time or interest in detailed or nuanced involvement, we're left with little more than a litany of pics, blurbs, and discreet, disconnected moments we now call *trends*.

We apply none of the attributes of reading to, well, what we read: no pause for consideration or even mere following an argument (remember, brief is better since we have no time to spare), no thoughtful follow-on beyond the occasional flaming of comments that are also worded to say as much as possible without saying much at all. And then we're done.

We see and share but we don't necessarily *care*, and people today rarely act upon the trends to which they've spent a fraction of their interest. Trends used to link *yesterday* with *today* and *tomorrow*, providing context for our interests and actions, thereby attaching consistent, continuous meaning to what we understood. But there's no way we can see or understand what trends are underway or happening around us when we're stuck in a constant state of **right now**, looking at ourselves for clues to what should matter. It's a prison as limiting as the visual stimuli on which it is based.

The only trend that is readily apparent is that there are no trends anymore, and to those symbols we defer upon bended knee.

WORDS

Do you really want to live in a world defined by images and visual symbols? It's how our ancestors lived, and it works just fine for all of the animal species that share our planet with us. Our genetics make us predisposed to its lure. It's also how today's technology and culture *want* you to live. We are encouraged, enabled, and then lauded for doing so both by our social institutions and our biology.

And, let's face it, reading can be chore. There's nothing inherently good or satisfying to it, any more than there is to putting a fork full of food to your mouth or plugging your earbuds into your smartphone. It's just a *behavior* and, unlike eating or listening to music, it requires a lot of front-end work, delays gratification in terms of what and when what you're reading will pay off, and gives no guarantee that it'll be rewarding whatsoever. Recent stats reveal that more than half of the entire American population will never open a book during this year. I'm surprised the number isn't higher, considering all of the immersive and more immediately satisfying mediated experiences available to us.

Words just take too much time...to write, to read, or to interpret in anything but short bursts of text, ideally 140 characters' worth or less. There's too much else to do.

Yet words are the only tool for communicating complete thoughts or ideas, the best mechanism for reaching collaborative understanding, and the last defense we have against the tyranny of those who'd like to limit our perception, manage our experience, and dictate our actions, whether purposefully or simply by default.

Images and other visual stimuli are imperfect vessels for communicating. They require interpretation of content that is literally framed by edges that exclude any additional information. Images, whether static or moving, are moments presented to viewers that prompt visceral, usually emotional responses. They contain no inherent or objective meaning, or at least little beyond what's most basic or blunt. That's why preliterate societies relied on visual symbols to define the authority of their religions and governing institutions. We, like other animals, are wired to react to images in immediate and simple ways. We run. We feel safe. We obey. As such, there is little way to argue with these expressions of power.

Words, and then writing, gave people tools by which they could literally talk about things, first in-person and then over distances of time and space. Literate societies were able to articulate and then share ideas about what they believed and how they wanted to live. Words made conversation possible, and conversations meant that people could learn from one another. At its very basic form, conversations are commerce, since ideas are transacted. The premise of advertising, just like speech overall, was to explain and inspire by giving would-be customers a better understanding of what was for sale. What people gave up in simplicity of belief they gained in comprehension of the world around them.

The 21st century finds us retreating from this empowerment. Political institutions and commercial brands are happy to communicate with their publics in videos and short bursts of copy. Like media theorist Marshall McLuhan explained, they find greater value in facilitating the behavior of engagement with the various social technologies now available than in the substance of what is communicated. We consumers are all too happy to oblige them this approach, since we're too busy to spend much time in thoughtful contemplation anyway. Better to get our information quickly and, ideally, pre-distilled and reviewed so we can simply *buy*, *pin*, or *forward* it.

There are any number of voices telling us this is a good thing, and that it is an improvement over the old days of limits on what was communicated and who did the communicating. We are encouraged to express ourselves in words without any of the requirements that reading and reasoned argument used to impose. Everyone has an equally valid opinion about everything, and anything shared is worth sharing unless the marketplace says otherwise. This reduces our use of written expression to resemble the visual: brief glimpses of content are vague because they say so little with even less authority. Our experience is supposed to be to react instead of internalize and truly respond.

We are encouraged to talk without saying much, while favoring the propagation of content instead of its understanding. The trends and ideas that matter most as those that get forwarded and viewed the most. Imposing any judgment or limitations on this noise would smack of *elitism*, though we are convinced in our innate right (and ability) to pass off our gut reactions and opinions in lieu of the constraints of honest and open analysis. Conversation is an inherent good now, even if all we're doing is sharing videos of cute kitties.

We have yet to find our voices in the 21st century.

There are exceptions to these circumstances, and they are very encouraging. Maybe you use reasoned arguments when you talk with the people who are most important to you in your life. Perhaps you expect the same from them, too. It's possible that the commercial brands you truly value and trust are those that take the time to explain things to you. You may have reached your political conclusions based on the same criteria.

But consider how many times you've defaulted to the quicker and easier utility of visual stimuli when you communicate, and substituted imagery when you meant to discover and understand meaning. I do it all the time. We all do, because we can't help it. It often times feels not only good but *right.*

It's wrong, unfortunately, because every day that passes in which you and I don't require or test reasoned arguments from the people and institutions around us, we risk abdicating our own authority and giving up the control of how and what we communicate. Each time we rely on imagery or visual stimuli to reach even the simplest or smallest conclusions, it's very possible that we're defaulting to what someone or something else wants us to do.

We need words to keep their intentions honest, just as we need them to check our own.

We need a Thousand Word Manifesto.

EPILOGUE:
THE THOUSAND WORDS MANIFESTO

THE THOUSAND WORDS MANIFESTO

Words are the software code for the computer that is society.

When we use less of them, either to express ourselves or understand one another, we give up our right to use society as a tool for our accomplishments and fulfillment, and ask it to use us as consumers and its servants.

Society's tools are imagery and symbols; its techniques are to substitute brief, vague, and incomplete visuals for reasoned arguments; and the habits it encourages are for us to react emotionally and share our visceral opinions. The noise of its multimedia richness is intended to keep us unfocused and impatient, while offering us ways to get evermore distracted with better and more frequent multitasking. It exploits our genetic predisposition to interact with visual and other direct sensory inputs. It feels easy, fast, and good to get asked to do nothing but comment on everything, and to exert the power to *buy* instead of struggle to understand *why*.

It tells us to forget detail, nuance, or shared understanding of anything but the most blunt emotions. A picture is worth a thousand words.

But we still possess the code. We know that words are the keys to blowing up our obedience to power and authority, and replacing it with conversation among equals. The details of written communication allow us to understand each other, identify our differences when we don't, and collaborate on subsequent action. Reading gives us the psychological space to comprehend, ponder, and then express ideas, not just emotions. Every species reacts to stimuli. We're better than that because we can talk.

No two people looking at the same image or video would write the same description of what it meant. A jargon-filled tweet often says less than its 140-character limit would allow, and a "like" or forward says something vague about a reaction or opinion without saying much at all. Brands that market to us entertaining online content tell us more about the creative agencies they hire than they reveal about their businesses. Institutions that rely on short bursts of finely-crafted information while ignoring the messy questions we're asking don't just leave us wanting, they insult our intelligence as they attempt to manipulate us. And they do harm to our world thereby.

We demand *more*.

More transparency. More substantive conversations. More acknowledgment of reality, and more sincere efforts to address it. More communication that informs us. More detail, and more time to consider it.

We demand more of *ourselves*.

More effort to explain to one another what we think and believe, not just presenting what we've been told as unalterable truth. More time spent listening than talking, and more sharing real insights instead of impromptu reactions. More focus on getting good at some things instead of passing judgment on everything. When presented with blunt symbols intended to manipulate or silence us, we will take back control and speak out.

We will fight the tyranny of brief, vague, and incomplete with the populism of detailed, specific, and finished. We'll do it with words, using a thousand words for every picture if we have to. The computer that is society belongs to us.

We own the code, and we will use it.

www.ingramcontent.com/pod-product-compliance
Lightning Source LLC
Chambersburg PA
CBHW020506030426
42337CB00011B/257